D1565007

Simple
Sermons
for
Saints
and
Sinners

W. Herschel Ford

BAKER BOOK HOUSE
Grand Rapids, Michigan 49506

Copyright 1954 by Zondervan Publishing House
Grand Rapids, Michigan

Reprinted 1986 by Baker Book House
Grand Rapids, Michigan
with the permission of the copyright holder

ISBN: 0-8010-3522-8

Fifth printing, August 1990

Printed in the United States of America

*This book is dedicated to my be-*loved wife, Maybelle, my comrade down through the years, the sharer of all my joys and woes, the one who knows all about me and still loves me.

Introduction

There are many reasons why the Bible continues year after year to be the world's "best seller." This is so because with every reading of the Bible its truths grip the heart and soul of the reader with their freshness and stimulation.

Preaching also should always contain those same elements that will make every sermon fresh and stimulating. It should use the "things at hand" to enlighten, encourage and inspire the hearers. Our Master did this. Consider His message to the woman at Jacob's well on "the water of life," or His lesson to the disciples on "the field is the world" as they walked through the field of grain.

Dr. Ford in his book, "Simple Sermons For Saints and Sinners", uses this same approach with marked success. In his own inimitable way, with the skill of a jeweler, he places the precious gems of Divine truth in new mountings. Using modern incidents and current phrases, he thunders the call and challenge of Christ to men. Blessed indeed is the modern prophet of God who knows how to do this. Dr. Ford knows how!

This splendid new book is centered in Christ, saturated with scripture, and permeated with doctrinal soundness. It will inspire every one who reads it. It will spark the sermon preparation of every preacher who uses it.

J. D. GREY, D.D.
Former President,
Southern Baptist Convention

Contents

1

Simply Out of this World

Blessed be the Lord God, the God of Israel, who only doeth wondrous things (Ps. 72:18).

The young people of today sometimes use expressive language. We often hear them say that some thing or some person is "simply out of this world." A girl meets a certain boy, and the next day she says to her friend: "He is absolutely marvelous — he is simply out of this world." One of them has a meal in a new restaurant and then exclaims, "The food was divine — it was simply out of this world!" In telling about a party which they have attended, they will say, "I had a wonderful time — everything was simply out of this world." What do they mean by this expression? They mean that the thing they are describing is extraordinary, wonderful, unique, unusual, something seldom seen in this world.

Now our young people mean well, but some of the things they call "out of this world" are quite ordinary after all. But not so with God! All that He does is wonderful, extraordinary, unusual, and "simply out of this world." The text says that the "Lord God . . . only doeth wondrous things." Let us look at a few of these things today.

I. THE SALVATION THAT GOD OFFERS IS SIMPLY OUT OF THIS WORLD

One day God looked down upon the world. He saw men wandering as sheep without a shepherd. They had no peace in their hearts, no purpose in their lives, no hope in their

7

souls. He looked upon them as they went over the precipice of death and down to their doom below. Then He looked at the great books of heaven and saw our names written there. Above each name were the words, "The soul that sinneth, it shall die — the wages of sin is death." Below our names He saw the long record of our sins. He knew that, according to His own great unchanging laws, we were lost. His compassionate heart was moved and He said, "I must do something about it."

And, oh, what a marvelous thing He did do! He perfected what we call the plan of salvation. The world has seen many great plans. We have had a plan to feed the starving nations. We have had a plan to win the war. We have had a plan of economic recovery. But there never has been a plan like God's plan of salvation. God knew that if He was to be a just God someone must pay the penalty of sin. This penalty must be paid by the sinner or by a substitute. So out of His great love He said, "I will choose a substitute." Now this substitute had to be one without sin, so that he could go and bear all the sins of mankind.

Oh, friends, there was only One who could measure up to this standard, there was only One who was absolutely perfect! It was God's own and Only-begotten Son. God loved Him and did not want to give Him up, but "God so loved the world that he gave his only begotten Son." When He presented the matter to His son, I am sure that the Son was in perfect agreement. "I, too, have seen the plight of sinful men," the Saviour must have said. "My heart has also been moved. Father, I will go down into the world and give my life away that they might live." So He came, He pierced the blue of the sky, He sped by the sun and the moon and the stars. He came into this old sinful world. After thirty-three and a half years of a marvelous life, He laid down that life for us all on Calvary's Cross: "Greater love hath no man than this, that he give his life for his friends."

What is our part of this plan? Must we pay some huge sum in order to be saved? Must we do some great thing? No. God tells us only to turn our back upon sin and to trust Christ. Then our sins will be forgiven and everlasting life will be ours. I tell you the salvation that He offers is simply out of this world. And "thanks be unto God," everyone of us can enjoy it. You may not be rich in the goods of this world, but if you have this salvation you have everything.

Martin Luther went to sleep one night troubled by his sin. In a dream he saw a recording angel standing at a big blackboard. Martin Luther's name was on this blackboard and the angel was making a list of all of Luther's sins. They were so many and so great that Martin Luther felt he could never be forgiven. But while he shuddered in despair, he saw a pierced hand writing above the list of sins these words, "The blood of Jesus Christ His Son cleanses from all sin." As he gazed in wonder the blood trickled down from the wounded hand and washed the record clean. Luther woke up, rejoicing, knowing that his sins had been forgiven.

Is it not wonderful? Have your sins been washed away? Oh, I tell you, the salvation, that He offers is simply out of this world.

II. The Holy Spirit and His Work
are Simply Out of This World

It might be well to say that the Holy Spirit is God's representative on earth, working in the hearts of men; but He is more than that. The Holy Spirit is God Himself and the work that He does is God's own work. The first thing that He does is to convict of sin. He makes men see their lost, sinful, ruined condition. Then He points men to the source of help. First he casts men down, and then He lifts them up. He says, "You are a sinner and you are lost." Then He says, "Yonder on Calvary is the Man who died for you. Look unto Him and be saved."

If the Holy Spirit did not convict us and point us to Christ, where would we be? We would be lost without knowing it; we would be on the way to doom without realizing it. We thank the man who points out our danger to us and shows us the way of escape. Let us thank the Holy Spirit for convicting us of sin and pointing us to the Saviour.

Now, when the soul responds to the voice of the Spirit, when sin is cast out, when the heart is opened up to Jesus, in that very minute the Holy Spirit comes to live forever in that heart. We often crowd Him into the tiny corners; we often grieve Him; we often stifle His voice; but He never, never leaves us.

He is there helping us in the time of sorrow. My phone rang the other morning, and the voice of one of my members came over the wire, telling me that a certain man had died during the night. I went right over to the home. The living room was filled with friends, and on one side sat the broken-hearted wife. The husband had died suddenly during the night. I talked with her a while, then offered a prayer. When I arose to leave she said, "You have brought great comfort to my heart." What had I done? I had done little, but the Holy Spirit had come to touch her heart and comfort her in her grief. He caused her to see that "all things work together for good to them that love God."

Do you remember that hour when your baby slipped away? Do you remember when that other loved one died? You thought that your heart would break. You felt that you could not go on; you were just about to give up. Then you heard a still small voice saying, "I will never leave thee, nor forsake thee." Somehow you were able to say, "It is all right. God's way is the best way after all. I will just trust Him and follow Him." It was the voice of the Holy Spirit, and as He spoke it seemed that you could feel the loving Father's arms about you.

Bishop Hughes was the pastor of a Boston church that had eight hundred members. When he had been there for two years, someone asked him to preach a sermon on comfort. He wondered how much this sermon was needed. So he took the church roll and listed all the families who had suffered some grief or trouble during those two years. He found that eighty per cent of his people needed this comfort. Sooner or later, sorrow comes to us all, but we have the Holy Spirit to comfort us in a way that is simply out of this world.

The Holy Spirit is there to strengthen. As we face the tasks of life we realize how weak we are in our own strength. We cry out with Paul, "Who is equal to these things?" We go out to fight our battles alone, and we meet defeat. We say, "Oh, Lord, I am but a little child, help me now!" It is then that He sends the Heavenly Power into our hearts. The preacher, the teacher and the singer can get that help — but they are not the only ones. That help is for the business man, the housewife, the school teacher, the professional man, the laboring man. That promise of help is open to every believer.

The Holy Spirit is there to guide. Life is full of cross-roads. We stand at these crossroads and wonder which direction we should take. Jesus said, "The Holy Spirit will guide you." And He does guide. Listen to Proverbs 3:6: "In all thy ways acknowledge him, and he shall direct thy paths." Put him first in everything, call upon Him when you need guidance, and it will surely be given to you. James 1:5: "If any of you lack wisdom, let him ask of God, that giveth to all men liberally, and upbraideth not; and it shall be given him."

Not only will He guide us in our choices, but in our attitudes. You will remember that Saul hounded David for many years, seeking to kill him. After Saul died, David became king. His friends said to him, "This is your chance to get even with Saul. You remember how he embarrassed and humiliated you; now you can take it out upon his family." But instead of adopting that attitude, David said, "If there is anyone left of Saul's family, find him for me, and I will show him kindness." They found that Saul had a crippled grandchild. David took him in and lovingly cared for him the rest of his life. That was the Christian attitude. If we let the Holy Spirit have His way in our hearts, He will guide us into a Christian attitude.

Yes, when the Holy Spirit convicts us and points us to the Saviour, when He comforts us in our sorrow, when He strengthens us in our weakness, when He guides us along life's pathway, we must say, "There is nothing like it — the Holy Spirit is simply out of this world."

III. The Bible is Simply Out of This World

One Thursday night I had the great privilege of leading a naval commander to Christ. He was baptized into the fellowship of our church and became active for the Lord. In a testimonial meeting one night, he said, "I knew that I needed to be a Christian and so I began to read the books of certain men. I thought that I could read myself into salvation, but in those books I found only the doubts and the theories of the authors. I had failed to read the Bible, the one book that can show a man the way of salvation." When this man was shown the Biblical way, he yielded immediately and became a child of God. Because of what the Bible can do for men I say that it is simply out of this world.

The Bible is out of this world in many other ways. It is

unusual in authorship, for God is the author of this book. He moved upon the hearts of men, causing them to pen its wonderful words. It is unusual in structure. There are sixty-six books in the Bible, written by forty authors over a period of fifteen hundred years. Yet every part fits perfectly into the whole book. It is unusual in its content. The Bible is preeminently the story of Jesus Christ. The Old Testament points to Him; the New Testament reveals Him. The Bible begins in the Garden of Eden where man lost Paradise through sin; it ends in the Garden of Heaven where Paradise is regained through a Saviour. It begins with God creating a world and putting man down into it; it ends with God bringing that man back home to live with Him forever.

When I was a boy my family was poor and needed many things. But I had a vivid imagination, and I often wished for a magic pocketbook. I wanted to open this pocketbook in the morning, and find a ten dollar bill in it, close it up, then open it the next morning and find another bill ready for spending. Now this never could happen, but the Bible is like that pocketbook. We open it up and take some valuable truth from it, then we close it again. We open it the next day and take out another valuable truth. Yet it is never exhausted. Yes, the Bible is one book that is simply out of this world.

IV. THE WAY GOD ANSWERS PRAYER IS SIMPLY OUT OF THIS WORLD

We sit in our homes and talk over a telephone around the world. We send a message by telegraph and in a few minutes that message is being read a thousand miles away. We speak over the radio and someone hears us ten thousand miles away. But before the telephone, the telegraph or the radio were dreamed of, God said, "Speak unto me and I will answer from my throne." Yes, it is wonderful that you and I can enter into the secret place, fall upon our knees and pray, and realize that someone is listening. Then it is more wonderful when later on we see in some public place that our request has been granted.

A godly farmer had two unsaved sons. Each morning before he went to the field to work, he knelt upon the floor of his barn and poured out his heart to God for the salvation of his boys. Often the boys would find him there; then they would nudge each other, smile and quietly go away. One day the old man died. A few days later, when the boys were cleaning up the barn, they found two grooves in the floor. It was there that their father had often planted his knees and cried out, "Oh, God, save my boys!" The two boys put away their brooms and fell upon their knees in the place where their father had prayed so often. "O God," they prayed, "for years father prayed for us, but his prayers were not answered while he was living. Now we come in simple faith to give our hearts to Christ." They were both saved that day.

Yes, God answers prayer. Sometimes He says, "No," sometimes He delays the answer for our own good, but He does answer. The way He answers is simply out of this world.

V. The Joy of Serving Christ Is Simply Out of This World

We often read of the hobbies which various people have, of the many things they do to get a thrill out of life. They search everywhere for happiness, never realizing that the greatest happiness and the highest joy in life come from serving Christ. They join some organization and when they are elected to an office in that organization, they get some joy out of it They are appointed chairman of some committee and get their pictures in the paper, and this brings them some joy. They serve on the winning team in some drive and get some joy from that victory. But none of these things can compare with the joy of knowing that you are doing something for Christ and His cause. That brings a thrill which is simply out of this world. God wants us to love people and bring them to Him. Men have sinned against God; they have crucified Christ. But God still loves them and He wants us to put our arms around them and invite them to Him. When we get busy in that kind of service, we find that it is simply out of this world.

VI. THE HEAVENLY HOME THAT HE HAS PREPARED IS SIMPLY OUT OF THIS WORLD

God knows about the trouble that we have in this world. He knows our sorrows, He sees our tears, He knows when we are blue and when our hearts are aching. He knows about our financial troubles, our domestic troubles, our personality troubles. He knows it all, so He says, "I will let my children live down there for a while and then I will bring them up here where none of these things can ever come."

The land He prepared for us is surely out of this world. Jesus said, "I go to prepare a place for you." The place is already prepared for us, but here is the question, "Are you prepared for that place?" There is only one way of preparation. Some people think they will get to heaven because they are church members, some because they are baptized, some because they partake of the Lord's Supper, some because they go through certain religious forms, some because of their works, some because of their gifts. But Christ says, "I am the way." The only way to come to God and to reach heaven is by the way of the Cross. You can get to heaven without wealth, without health, without friends, without influence; but you can never get to heaven without Christ. The minute you trust Him you are on the way to heaven. When life is ended you will be home forever.

We are on the way to the "land that is fairer than day." We are "bound for the Promised Land." Its "builder and maker is God." The sweet chariot will soon swing low and take us home. When we get there and see all that God has prepared for us, we will exclaim with one of old, "The half was not told me."

A great baseball player lay dying. He had been a wonderful Christian and he loved the Lord. Some of the other players stood by his bedside and he said to them, "Boys, I have played my last game, but I have signed up on the All-star team up above. Get on that team, boys, she's a winner!" Are you on that team, my friend? If you are, you are going to a place that is simply out of this world.

Why are all of these things so wonderful? Why are they simply out of this world? *It is all because of Jesus.* If it were **not** for Him there would be no salvation, the Holy Spirit would mean nothing to us, prayer would be an empty thing, the Bible would be a dead book, there would be no joy in service, there would be no heavenly home at the end of the way. Ah, yes, if Jesus is yours, if He fills your heart, everything wonderful in this world and the next is yours.

Irvin Cobb tells the story of an old doctor who was a fine Christian and a useful man. He did not have a swanky office. He had only two or three small rooms on the second floor of a building, at the head of a flight of steps. On the street below was this sign, "Dr. Thomas Riley—Office Upstairs." One day the doctor was missing. They found him dead in his office. A few nights before, he had gone out into a snowstorm on a call. He had then taken cold and died. When his friends buried him they wanted to perpetuate his memory in the best way. They wondered what sort of stone to put over his grave, and what epitaph to put on the stone. They thought of his labors of love and how he had gone on up to heaven. So one of his friends took the old battered sign and put it upon the doctor's grave. It simply said, "Dr. Thomas Riley — Office Upstairs," and pointed toward heaven.

If Jesus is our Saviour, when the end comes, we, too, can go upstairs and be at home with God. When we get there, when we see Him face to face, when we know that all the joys of heaven are awaiting us, then we will surely say, "It is true — the Lord God only doeth wondrous things."

2

No Greater Sin

He that believeth on the Son hath everlasting life: and he that believeth not the Son shall not see life; but the wrath of God abideth on him (John 3:36).

What is the greatest sin in the world? Some will say that it is murder. Yet Paul, who was responsible for the murder of many Christians, was saved and in turn became a remarkable Christian. The crucifiers of Christ were murderers, but it is probable that many of them were saved on the day of Pentecost. The Bible tells us that there will be no murderers in heaven; but some who have been murderers will be there, their souls saved and their sins washed away in the blood of Christ.

Some will say that theft is the greatest sin, but the thief on the cross heard Jesus saying to him, "To day shalt thou be with me in paradise." Some thieves go to prison, hear the Gospel and are saved. There will be no thieves in heaven, but those who have been thieves and who have had their sins forgiven will be there. Some will say that adultery is the greatest sin. Yet Jesus forgave the woman who was taken in that sin. And the woman who had five husbands and was still living in adultery was saved after a wonderful interview with Him at the well near Sychar. There are no adulterers in heaven, but many who have committed this grievous sin will be there, having had a remarkable experience of salvation through Jesus Christ.

But what is the greatest sin in the world? It is simply the rejection of the Lord Jesus Christ. Are you a sinner? God loves you; He gave His Son to die upon Calvary's Cross for you. Now He offers this wonderful salvation to you. He offers to save you for this life and for the life that is to come. You may reject that Lovely One, you may trample Him under foot, you may do nothing with Him and live without any thought of Him; but in so doing you have committed the greatest sin and you will pay the highest price for your rejection. Now what does a man do when he rejects Christ?

I. In Rejecting Christ a Man Shuts the Door to His Own Highest Possibilities

God has a great question in His Book. It is this: "What shall I do with Jesus, who is called Christ?" Until you have said "yes" to Jesus you cannot possibly rise to the highest possibilities of your own life. No man is at his best until he has linked his own possibilities to the power of Christ.

Someone asked a great man this question: "How may I become successful?" This was the answer he received: "Link your life to a great cause and give your best to that cause." Find a man who is doing the most good for God and the world, and you will find a man who has linked his life to that of Christ. Oh, how many useless people there are in the world! They are people who are making no contribution to the world, simply because they have not linked their lives with Jesus.

In the old days in Pennsylvania a little shop stood by the side of a great factory. The little shop had small power, but the great factory had all of its machinery running and still had power which was going to waste. The owner of the little shop said to the owner of the factory, "Let me break through the wall between my little shop and your factory and let me place one of my belts on your great wheel so that I might use some of this power which is going to waste." The owner of the great factory permitted him to do this, and soon the little shop, with this added power, became a great factory.

You are like the little shop — your power is small; but Jesus, who has all power in heaven and in earth, says to you, "Link on to Me and use My power." So if you will cut loose from sin and surrender to Him, His power will be your power; you can rise to your highest possibilities. But if you reject Him and hold on to your sin and the world, you will be hindered from rising to your best.

II. IN REJECTING CHRIST A MAN PUTS HIMSELF IN THE WAY OF OTHERS

Sometime ago I went out into the yard on a moonlit night, for I knew that soon there would be an eclipse of the moon as predicted by the astronomers. I looked up and saw the shadow of the sun moving across the moon. The shadow became larger and larger until the moon was entirely blotted out. Well, yonder is Christ, the Light of the World. Someone is looking at you. If you are not a Christian, you become a shadow moving between that someone and Christ. You cut the onlooker off from His blessed light. No man goes to heaven or hell alone. You have an influence on someone. Someone is following your example. Are you lifting that some one up or pulling him down?

It has been my great sorrow to know many parents who stood in the way of their children. Some of those parents were not Christians at all. Some had formerly been active for Christ, but came to live backslidden lives. They had married, and children had come; they had stayed away from God's House; they had drifted into the world; their lives stood in the way of their children. When a baby is born it ought to be a time for the parents to rededicate themselves anew to God. They should say, "Here is a new life for which I am responsible. I must live for God so that my influence will be a blessing to this child." If you are not a Christian, you stand in the way of others.

Dr. George W. Truett tells about a certain meeting he once held. Every night a fine sixteen-year-old boy was at the meeting and seemed to be deeply interested. The preacher said to him one night, "I notice that you have been interested in the services. Why don't you come to Christ?" The boy replied, "My father is a doctor. He never goes to church. He is not a Christian and he is the finest man I know. I am going to follow him. He says by his example that the Christian religion isn't worthwhile."

The next morning the preacher found his way to the doctor's office and said to him, "I want to talk to you about your boy. I have never known a finer boy, but I am worried about him. He has been to our meeting and is interested in the salvation of his soul, but now he has put the matter aside. I talked to him last night and he told me that you were his example, that he was going to follow in your footsteps, which would mean that he would not become a Christian. Doctor, you owe something to this boy; you have too much at stake to let this matter go by." The doctor's face clouded and he said, "That is the heaviest blow I ever received. When will you have your next service?" And the preacher replied, "We meet again tonight at eight o'clock." "I will be there," said the doctor; "I know just what to do."

The doctor came that night. He listened to the sermon and when the invitation was given he walked down the aisle and made his surrender to Christ. As the preacher took his hand he said, "Doctor, look behind you!" As the doctor turned about he saw his fine son coming down the aisle to make the same surrender. The boy threw his arms around the father's neck and said, "Oh, Daddy, I am so glad you came! I wanted to be a Christian and now you have made it so much easier for me."

Oh, if you are not living as you should for Christ, think of the others upon whom you cast a shadow. Are you standing in their way?

III. In Rejecting Christ a Man Puts Himself on the Devil's Side

If you reject Christ you are taking the side of the Devil. There is no middle ground: you are either on Christ's side or Satan's side. If you reject Christ, you and your influence are on the side of the evil one.

There are millions of Christians in America. If they were on the right side in every moral question, we would not be harrassed by the liquor traffic nor the other deadly things of our American life. We would not only vote the wrong things out, we would vote the right men in. Our laws would be enforced and we would live in a better land. There are enough Christians in this country to clean it up once and for all if they took Christ's side on every moral issue. When these questions arise you ought to say, "If Jesus were here what stand would He take?" Then get on the side that you know He would be on and stand, even though all the heavens fall. But, if you reject Christ, you are putting yourself on the wrong side — on the Devil's side.

IV. In Rejecting Christ a Man Insults God

God is a great Father. He loves every creature in the world. Yet He knows you are lost and bound for hell. So in His great love He says, "I will save you, and I will help you, even though it may cost me my Only-begotten Son. I will give Him up freely for you." So He gives His Son to die upon the Cross for you. If you turn your back upon Him, if you reject Him, you are saying, "Away with Him, away with God, I care nothing for Him or His Son." That is an insult to Almighty God. If you continue in this course there is no hope for you.

You have heard of the atheist who flaunts himself in the face of God and says, "If there be a God let Him strike me down." You shudder when you hear about this and you say that the man is insulting God. But wait a minute. Have not you done something worse than this? You are an intelligent person, you hear the Gospel, you know that there is a God and that He gave His Son to die for you. If you reject Him, your insult is worse than the blasphemy of the most blatant infidel.

V. In Rejecting Christ a Man
Crucifies the Son of God Afresh

No man ever suffered as did Christ upon the Cross. His was a threefold suffering — physical, mental and spiritual. Since He took upon Calvary the anguish of sinners, He surely must have suffered as much on the Cross as a lost man would suffer in hell. Now that suffering and that sacrifice were for every man. "He is the propitiation for our sins, and not for our sins only, but for the whole world." His suffering therefore was for those who accept Him and in like manner for those who reject Him. When a man rejects Christ, he crucifies the Son of God afresh.

VI. In Rejecting Christ a Man Rejects
the Testimony of the World's Greatest Men

John the Baptist said, "Behold the Lamb of God, which taketh away the sin of the world."

Paul said, "In him dwelleth all the fulness of the Godhead bodily."

Peter said, "Thou art the Christ, the Son of the living God."

Nicodemus said, "Rabbi, we know that thou art a teacher come from God."

Polycarp said, "Eighty and six years have I served Him, and He has done me nothing but good."

Tolstoi said, "For thirty-five years of my life I was a man who believed in nothing. Five years ago my faith came to me. I believed in Jesus, and my whole life underwent a sudden transformation. Life and death ceased to be evil. Instead of despair I tasted joy and happiness."

Gladstone said, "All that I think, all that I hope, all that I write, all that I live for, is based on the Divinity of Jesus Christ, the central joy of my poor, wayward life."

J. P. Morgan said, "I commit my soul into the hands of my Saviour, in full confidence that having redeemed it and washed it in His most precious blood, He will present it faultless before the throne of my Heavenly Father."

Browning said, "If a man plucked even a rag from the body of Jesus and wore it in contempt — despite self, he would look greater and be better."

In my library I have a book with the title *Greatest Thoughts About Jesus Christ.* In this book thousands of men pay their tribute to the Saviour. I have not space to quote these tributes to you, but all of them testify to the wonders that are in Christ Jesus. If you reject Christ, you are taking your stand against the greatest men who ever lived, for all of the truly great men have been Christians

VII. In Rejecting Christ a Man Seals His Doom in Hell Forever

Psalm 9:17: "The wicked shall be turned into hell, and all the nations that forget God."

Isaiah 14:9: "Hell from beneath is moved for thee to meet thee at thy coming . . ."

John 3:18: "He that believeth on him is not condemned: but he that believeth not is condemned already, because he hath not believed in the name of the only begotten Son of God."

John 3:36: "He that believeth on the Son hath everlasting life: and he that believeth not the Son shall not see life; but the wrath of God abideth on him."

Revelation 14:10: "The same shall drink of the wine of the wrath of God, which is poured out without mixture into the cup of his indignation; and he shall be tormented with fire and brimstone . . ."

Revelation 20:15: "And whosoever was not found written in the book of life was cast into the lake of fire."

Revelation 21:8: "But the fearful, and unbelieving, and the abominable, and murderers, and whoremongers, and sorcerers, and idolaters, and all liars, shall have their part in the lake which burneth with fire and brimstone . . ."

Here is a man made in the image of God. He is a man with wonderful possibilities in his life. God recognizes these possibilities and gives him every possible opportunity to be saved—through the Church and through the Bible and through the Holy Spirit and through the Gospel He calls him to eternal life. But that man feels sufficient unto himself. He goes his way rejecting Christ and leaving God out. He goes his way holding on to his sin. What does this man have waiting for him at the end of the way when Christ takes the upper hand? *The Answer: Nothing but Doom.*

One day an outdoor preacher preached a sermon on hell.
A heckler in his audience cried out, "Where is hell?" And
the preacher wisely answered back: "Hell is at the end of
a Christless life." It is true: in rejecting Christ a man seals
his doom in hell forever.

In a small town in Texas a revival meeting was being held
under a brush arbor. The crowds were coming, and many souls
were being saved. One of the deacons of the church had a
son who was deaf and dumb. Someone came to the singer
and said to him, "Dummy Walker wants to come down the
aisle and give his heart to Christ." "How do you know?"
asked the singer, "He cannot talk." The man replied, "Today,
when no one else was here, he came into the meeting place,
put his hand on his heart, pointed to the setting sun and then
walked down the aisle. He sat down on the mourner's bench
and then walked over to the pulpit and patted the Bible. He
then shook hands with himself and pointed again to the sun
as if he were saying that when the sun went down he would
come down the aisle and give his heart to Christ."

The preacher and the singer went out to Dummy's home immediately. They found him and said to him, "Dummy, do
you want to be saved? Do you want to be a Christian?" He
opened his mouth and gave out an awful sound, but they could
not understand what he meant. They took him to his father
and the preacher asked, "Deacon, can you tell Dummy about
accepting Christ?" The deacon replied, "Preacher, I am
fifty-three years of age. I have been a Christian since I
was eleven and a deacon since I was thirty. I can tell Dummy
anything about the farm and he will understand, but I cannot tell him about Christ. Maybe his mother can help."

The trio then went into the kitchen, and the preacher said
to the mother: "Dummy wants to give his heart to Christ. Can
you tell him about the Saviour?" The tears came into her

eyes, and she said, "I am forty-eight years of age. I have been a Christian since I was nine. I can tell Dummy to bring in the wood and he understands it. I can tell him to call his father and he understands. I have tried to make him understand about Christ, but I have failed. Maybe his sister can help him. She is out in the garden."

They went out into the garden and found the sister. The preacher said, "Dummy wants to give his heart to Christ. Can you tell him about the Saviour?" The sister walked over and put her arm around Dummy and said, "Preacher, I am twenty-seven years of age. My husband and I are both Christians. Since I was a child I have brought the Sunday school cards home to Dummy. I have tried to make him understand about Christ, but I cannot do it."

The preacher said, "There is only one thing for us to do —let us pray." They dropped upon their knees there in the garden and all of them prayed except Dummy.

That night the brush arbor was packed with people. The sermon was preached and the invitation was given. The first one to come down the aisle was Dummy. He knelt on the ground in front of the pulpit while the preacher bowed his head and wept. In a moment the preacher felt a tug at his coat. He looked up and Dummy was standing there with his face beaming. The poor boy raised his hands toward the skies as if to embrace the heavens, then brought his hands down to his heart. He did this again, pointing to the Bible and then to his heart. Then he reached out his hand to the preacher. A great smile wreathed his face, and the people voted to give him the hand of Christian fellowship. The saints of God began to shout, for again Jesus had wrought a miracle.

During the remaining days of the revival Dummy won more people to Christ than any of the others. He could not talk, but he would put his arms around a lost man, hug him to his heart and smile. Then he would point to the sky, then to the man's heart. Then he would give him a little shove down the aisle. One by one he led a score of souls to know Jesus Christ.

Oh, my friend, if a poor deaf and dumb boy needed Christ and wanted a Saviour, you need Him, too! Do you not want Him today? Do not go on rejecting Him — it will be tragic if you take this course. Accept Him as your Saviour, live for Him and know the greatest joy and happiness that can come to any soul.

3

Crucified Christians

I am crucified with Christ: nevertheless I live; yet not I, but Christ liveth in me: and the life which I now live in the flesh I live by the faith of the Son of God, who loved me, and gave himself for me (Gal. 2:20).

The Christian life is the noblest and happiest life that a man can live, but it is no bed of roses and no holiday journey. Once you enter this life it is a battle from that day until you rest in the haven of heaven. It is a demanding life; to live it rightly means a full and complete surrender to the will of God.

If I invite you to become a Christian and tell you that the Christian life is one long sweet song, I am deceiving you. Yet I would rather fight a good fight of faith and endure the toils along the way, having Christ as my daily portion, and find a place in heaven with Him at the end of the way, than to go along without Him, to enjoy all the fruits of sin, to gain the whole world, and to come to eternal death at the end of life's little day.

The text says: "I am crucified with Christ." What is meant by that? We know what it meant for Christ to be crucified. We see a Cross on a "green hill far away." Hanging on that Cross is the Son of God, dying not for His sin, but for the sin of others. The sun goes behind the clouds and we hear the cry, "My God, my God, why hast thou forsaken me?"

We see Him as He bows His head and gives up the ghost, and we hear another cry, "It is finished."

> See from His head, His hands, His feet,
> Sorrow and love flow mingled down;
> Did e'er such love and sorrow meet,
> Or thorns compose so rich a crown?

I understand that: I know what it meant for Christ to be crucified. But when Paul says, "I am crucified," what does he mean? He was not there; he did not hang on the Cross. What does he mean when he says, "I am crucified"?

Crucifixion means death. If we are crucified, we are dead to sin, to the old life, to the old lusts, to the old self, to the old ambitions. We take a stand over here with Christ, and we say to the sinful and worldly things over there, "So far as you are concerned I am dead. You have no more power over me than you can have over a dead body." Paul is saying a great thing here. He did not reach that standard in a day or a month. It was a long, hard process, and it will be hard for us, too. But in the fight we are promised the help of the same Saviour who walked by the side of Paul and who says to us, "Lo, I am with you alway."

God help us to say, "I am crucified with Christ." And here is the secret of being able to say that — listen to the last part of the verse: "nevertheless I live, yet not I, but Christ liveth in me." All things are possible to us if He is a living reality reigning on the throne of our hearts.

I. A Christian's Feet Should Be Crucified

Jesus' feet were crucified. They crossed His feet upon the upright beam of the Cross and drove the long spike into them. That spike tore through the flesh and the blood and the bones — just imagine the agony of it!

Our feet should be crucified, too. What do we mean by

"crucified feet"? Well, we must be careful where they take us and never let them lead us into a place that will dishonor Him. If our feet are crucified, we will be following in His wounded footsteps.

One night He washed the feet of His disciples: He wants our feet to be clean, too. They ought never to walk in the slimy places of this old earth, but on the contrary they ought to go on many errands of mercy. They ought to carry us to those who are needy and poor and lost. We are to use our feet in Christian service, offering help and salvation to our fellow men.

Now that means missions. Christ wants the Gospel to go to the ends of the earth, and some feet must go to take the message. Will you go? But you say you have never been called. Then He has called you to send others. Are you doing that? Are you helping in God's great redemptive program for the whole world?

Mercury was the messenger of the gods; his feet were winged feet. We are messengers of the Heavenly Father. If we are crucified with Christ our feet will never take us where sin's allurement is, but they will take us on many errands of mercy in the name of the King.

> Take my feet and let them be,
> Swift and beautiful for Thee.

II. A Christian's Hands Should Be Crucified

Jesus' hands were crucified. They were stretched out upon the crossbeam of that cruel Cross and in agony and blood they were nailed to the tree. Back in the upper room, He showed those hands to His disciples. Thomas looked upon the prints of the nails, crying, "My Lord and my God!"

If our hands are crucified, we will be careful what we handle. They should never handle anything that will stain them with sin or wrong. The blessed pierced hands of Jesus were laid upon suffering human beings to bless them, but can you imagine Jesus holding anything sinful in those hands? If you want to be like Him, you must be careful what your hands handle.

Jesus' hands would never hold anything tainted by dishonesty. I will tell you what He wants you to do with your hands. You are to labor, giving a good day's work, and then you are to take the money—the fruit of your honest toil—put aside His part for His work and lay your hands in blessing upon this old world's sorrow. Can you imagine Jesus handling a bottle of whiskey or some of the other things Christians carelessly handle today?

Oh, we are to be crucified Christians! And our hands ought to be dead to sin and wrong, and they ought to be active in the service of the King of kings because Christ is living in us.

III. A Christian's Ears Should Be Crucified

If our ears are crucified we will be careful about the things to which we listen. There are voices all about us, voices that tempt us downward; but if we are His, we will not listen to these voices.

Some of these are Sunday voices which say, "Don't go to God's house. You have been busy all the week. Have a good time. Do this thing or go to that place." That is the voice of the Devil, and the crucified Christian must not listen to him. Some of these voices are weekday voices. They say, "Put over a shady deal. Make more money. Follow the path of circumstances. Forget what the preacher said on Sunday. You must look out for yourself." Yet, we must be deaf to all these cries. They come from Satan and they lure us toward the gates of hell.

Crucified ears do not listen to gossip and the things which

hurt others. The one who listens is almost as bad as the one who tells. There are many who lap up gossip with their ears as a cat laps up milk with his tongue. They have "itching ears." They want to hear something detrimental about someone else, but they should never hear it from a crucified Christian.

I have never read that Jesus listened to gossip about anyone. If we are crucified Christians, we will say, "I am deaf to all that is wrong and hurtful; Christ liveth in me."

IV. A Christian's Eyes Should Be Crucified

Isaiah was talking about Jesus when he said, "His visage was marred more than any man." On the Cross His face must have been battered beyond recognition. They pressed the crown of thorns upon His brow. It pierced his eyebrows, and the blood covered His eyes. Yes, His eyes were crucified eyes.

If our eyes are to be crucified, we must be careful at what they look. There are so many things today that make an appeal to the eyes, and through the eyes to the lower passions. The world uses color and light to lure us downward. For proof of this go to the newsstand and look at the pictures there upon the various magazines. If our eyes are crucified we must look away from those things.

The motto of a certain preacher is, "Keep looking up." We are to look up for His coming. If we remember that He is coming to reward us according to our works, we will be busy for Him. Our eyes will look out upon the needs of the world. We will see that the fields are white unto the harvest, and we will not be content until we are gathering this harvest for Him.

In the Book of Hebrews is the phrase, "Looking unto Jesus." This is the best use in the world for the eyes. Some look to themselves: they need no one else; some look to others: they desire applause. The best thing to do is to look unto Jesus.

A Christian dreamed that he was deep in a well in the middle of the night, but as he looked up he saw a single star. He kept looking up, and it seemed that the star let down silver lines into the well to lift him up a bit. Then he looked down and immediately he began to sink. So he kept his eyes upon the star until finally he was lifted out of the well. There is just one star for the Christian — Jesus, the Bright and Morning Star. We are to keep looking up, for the upward look will lift our lives toward God.

V. A Christian's Tongue Should Be Crucified

James says some practical things about the tongue. He says that you can put bits in the mouths of horses to turn them, but that no one can turn the tongue. We turn a great ship in its course with a little rudder, but not so with the tongue. He tells us that fire is a destructive thing, but that the tongue burns quicker than any flame. He tells us that we can tame all manner of beasts, but that the tongue cannot be tamed.

Now if we use our tongues for Him, we will never wag them unnecessarily. Here is a prayer that all of us ought to pray: "Lord, help me to keep my mouth shut!"

I have seen it happen in a church. One tongue started wagging, then another and another. Soon the church was split to pieces, the work was hurt and the people were divided. The young people left the church and went out into the world, while the Devil laughed with glee. "Teach me, and I will hold my tongue" (Job 6:24).

We should not be glad when we hear evil things of some-one else, Certainly we do not have to repeat them. They might boomerang and do us more harm than the one about whom they were said.

There will be no sharp words from us if our tongues are crucified. There are some who delight in biting sarcasm. You meet them one day and they say a little thing that stings for a week. Our words should be soothing and not like salt on a wounded back.

VI. A Christian's Heart Should Be Crucified

Jesus' heart was crucified. Some say that He died of a broken heart, and no wonder. He came to His own and His own received Him not. The sin of the world was upon Him. Even God's back was turned for the time being. As He died they thrust the spear into His side, and water and blood gushed out. Yes, His heart was crucified.

Is your heart crucified? Is it dead to sin and evil? Is it a throne upon which He lives? Does He have first place in your life, or is your heart divided between the world and Jesus?

An old Saxon warrior united with the Church and came forward to be baptized. He told the minister to immerse every part of him except one hand. But he was told that the whole body was to be "buried with Christ." "No", said the warrior, "I want to keep this hand free to battle my enemies. I do not want it given to Christ." We are often like that. We give part of our lives to Christ and hold back the other part. But if we are crucified Christians, the whole heart is His. And that means the whole life belongs to Him.

During World War I a man from Sweden came before the American Draft Board. He was told that as an alien he could claim exemption, but he replied, "No, when I came to America, I came all. If America needs me, I am ready." That is the spirit we need. We need to say, "All of me belongs to Christ. If He needs me, I am ready."

If your heart is crucified you will have the right attitude in that heart. You will not go around with your feelings stuck out on your sleeves. A crucified man is a dead man, and a dead man has no feelings. Why should a Christian go around looking for someone to hurt his feelings? Let us be big people, let us have the right attitude; let us love others regardless of the circumstances.

In the history of France the Dreyfus case is outstanding. Dreyfus was arrested unjustly, given an unfair trial and sent to Devil's Island to suffer and die. But in France there was one man who believed in him. Zola, the author, worked for many years in his behalf. Zola lost position and fame and practically suffered ostracism because of his stand, but he finally won freedom for Dreyfus. Dreyfus came back to France. When Zola died sometime later, Dreyfus prepared to go to the funeral. His friends told him that he would be risking his life to go, but he replied, "I care not for the risk. Nothing shall keep me from showing I have a grateful heart in my bosom."

There was One who did more for us than Zola did for Dreyfus. We were sunk in the deep sea of sin. The law had us in its grip. No one believed in us. But He loved us; He gave up the glory of heaven and came down and died to save us. We ought to let nothing keep us from showing our gratitude to Him.

Our lives ought to be used for Him. He bought them with a price. When the crown of thorns was pressed upon His head, He bought your head, your eyes, your ears, your tongue. When the nails pierced His hands, He bought your hands with all their capacity to serve. When the nails pierced His feet, He bought your feet which ought always to be running errands of love for Him. When His great heart broke, He bought your heart with its capacity to love and serve. If Jesus lives in you, He ought to shine through you.

In the days of the Crusaders a certain Bishop decided to take some of the soil of Calvary back to his native land. Consequently fifty-three ships were laden with soil from the Holy Land, the soil was taken back to form a resting place for the dead in the old country. The next year a strange new flower appeared in this cemetery. The year following there were many more such flowers. As the years passed by, the wind blew the pollen from these flowers over all the country. Today at a certain season in that country, every hillside is covered with this beautiful flower. And if you ask the natives where this little flower originated, they will say, "It came from Calvary long, long ago."

God help us so to live and hide behind the Cross that people will say, "These things came from his life, not because of his personality or ability or learning, but because he has been to Calvary and has had a touch with Jesus." Let us go there today, let us leave all of our old sins and put aside all selfishness and worldliness and let us give ourselves afresh to the Saviour for today and for all the days to come, so that as we come away we can say, "I am crucified with Christ!"

4

Old Soldiers Never Die

For I am now ready to be offered, and the time of my departure is at hand. I have fought a good fight, I have finished my course, I have kept the faith: henceforth there is laid up for me a crown of righteousness, which the Lord, the righteous judge, shall give me at that day: and not to me only, but unto all them also that love his appearing (II Tim. 4:6-8).

Sometime ago General of the Army Douglas MacArthur was relieved as United Nations Commander in the Far East. Some people say that this was one of the former President's biggest mistakes. I never bring politics into my sermons. I do not know what would happen if MacArthur's policies were carried out in the Orient, but I do know this: MacArthur did a grand job in Japan. When he went to Japan, he said that the remaking of that nation was a "theological question." He felt that it was a matter of the Japanese getting right with God. He called on us for one thousand missionaries. We have not sent that many, but we have sent a large number, and some of the greatest revivals in modern history have been held in Japan. Because of MacArthur's matchless leadership and all the other contributing factors, Japan is a different country today. MacArthur deserves great praise for the work that he did over there.

When the General came back to America after fourteen years abroad, he made a speech to the Amercian Congress.

It was one of the finest and most dramatic speeches ever heard in America. At the end of the speech he quoted an old song of the Army, "Old Soldiers Never Die."

But I have not come today to talk to you about MacArthur; you can read about him in the newspapers and magazines. I want to tell you of another old soldier, an old soldier of the Cross. His name is Paul. As we meet him in II Timothy 4:6-8, he is coming down toward the end of the way and he says, "I am now ready to be offered, and the time of my departure is at hand. I have fought a good fight, I have finished my course, I have kept the faith: henceforth there is laid up for me a crown of righteouness, which the Lord, the righteous judge, shall give me at that day: and not to me only, but unto all them also that love his appearing." In a little while his head would roll off the block and they would pronounce him dead. But his soul, his spirit, the real Paul would be living on forever and ever with the Christ whom he loved. It is true that old soldiers of the Cross never die.

I. Paul Had a Great Career as a Soldier

There was a time when Paul hated Christ and the Cross. He fought against Christianity with all the zeal and fervor of his soul. But one day on the Damascus road the mighty Captain of Salvation halted him. Christ saved him and transformed him, and from that day on he became the greatest and most effective soldier Jesus ever had.

Paul was a strange man. When he gave his life to Christ who saved him, he felt that he ought to give all of himself to the Saviour. So he said that he was dead to the old life, and that he was living only for Christ. He said that a soldier did not entangle himself in the affairs of this world; for if a soldier did this he could not do his best as a soldier and he could not please his master.

Christians need to learn that lesson today. Too many of them are mixed up with the things of this world. Thus their powers become dissipated and they are not able to do anything for God. When we ask them to do something for the Lord and to be faithful to the Church, they tell us that they are too busy. When you are too busy to do something for God, you are busier than God wants you to be.

Paul also said that a soldier of the Cross must learn to endure hardness. He was certainly a worthy example of this great truth. When he came to Christ, his family and friends turned against him. Often he was placed in prison, many times he was beaten with stripes, he suffered the heat of the summer and the cold of the winter, he was shipwrecked three times, once he was stoned and left for dead. But he could say, "The Lord stood by me in it all." In spite of all that happened, he rejoiced to suffer for Christ's sake: "Therefore I take pleasure in infirmities, in reproaches, in necessities, in persecutions, in distresses for Christ's sake."

No man ever suffered for Christ as Paul did. Here is the list in II Corinthians 11:23: "In stripes above measure, in prisons more frequent, in deaths oft. Of the Jews five times received I forty stripes save one. Thrice was I beaten with rods, once was I stoned, thrice I suffered shipwreck, a night and a day I have been in the deep; in journeyings often, in perils of waters, in perils of robbers, in perils by mine own countrymen, in perils by the heathen, in perils in the city, in perils in the wilderness, in perils in the sea, in perils among false brethren, in weariness and painfulness, in watchings often, in hunger and thirst, in fastings often, in cold and nakedness. Beside those things that are without, that which cometh upon me daily, the care of all the churches."

Have we ever suffered anything for Christ? Have we ever made a sacrifice for Him? Paul did this and he calls on us to do the same thing: "I beseech you therefore, brethren, by the mercies of God, that ye present your bodies a living sacrifice, holy, acceptable unto God, which is your reasonable service" (Rom. 12:1).

Paul's life was marked by the highest loyalty to his great Commander in chief, the Lord Jesus Christ. On one occasion Latimer, the great Christian martyr of England, announced that he would preach on a subject forbidden by the king. Just as the service started, the king and his company entered and took their seats. When Latimer stood up to preach, he did a dramatic thing. He walked back and forth in the pulpit, saying, "Latimer, thy king heareth thee. Be careful what you say." Then he stopped at the pulpit, put his hand on the Bible, looked up to heaven, and said, "Latimer, thy Lord heareth thee. Be careful what you say." He then went on to preach the powerful sermon which he had prepared for that occasion. At the close of the service, the king came up and said to him, "God bless you, Latimer. I love and respect a man who fears God more than he fears his king." That was like Paul. He was loyal to Christ above everything and everyone else on earth.

II. THE OLD SOLDIER LOOKS BACK ON LIFE

"I have fought a good fight," Paul says. He looks upon life as a battle to be fought, a victory to be won. He said on one occasion that he was not fighting flesh and blood, but the evil hosts of Satan. That is a fight which never ends this side of glory.

In the first place, Paul had to fight himself. Writing to the Romans, Paul had said in effect, "I have been saved, but the old carnal nature is still present. I want to be absolutely free of sin, but I am having a desperate fight. There are two natures in me. The flesh and the spirit are both there, and

they are always fighting, the one against the other. The things
that I would do, I do not. The things that I ought not to do,
I do." But in his first letter to the Corinthians Paul tells where
the victory comes in: "Thanks be unto God, which giveth us
the victory through our Lord Jesus Christ."

We are just like that. We are surrounded by all sorts
of temptations. They are on the right of us, the left of us,
in front of us and behind us. We are bounded by temptations on the north, the south, the east and the west. We
often give in and let the Devil defeat us. Then we are miserable indeed. But on other occasions we pray and we overcome
temptations through the power of Christ. Then our hearts
are flooded with happiness.

Paul also had to fight the enemies of the Gospel. They
knew how faithful he was to Christ, so they tried in every
way to hinder him and to block his testimony for the Lord.
These enemies are still alive today. When we Christians
set out to make our lives count for Christ, these enemies get
busy and try to ruin our testimony. They say, "It's all right
to be a church member, but you shouldn't give so much time
to it. Come along with us." They say, "It won't hurt you to
miss prayer meeting one Wednesday night. Come along with
us." They say, "There is no harm in this. Everybody does it."
And many Christians give in. They soon go astray and lose
their witness.

Let me ask you this question: Did you ever see anyone who
had a great influence for God who did not put Christ and
His church first always? No, you never did. If you want to
be a maximum Christian, fight down every temptation to side-
step, set your face toward the goal and follow Him all the way.

At the end of his way, Paul says: "I have fought a good
fight." We will be able to say that, too, if we have lived
at our best for Christ.

Paul goes on to say, "I have finished my course." He looks upon life as a race track: "This is the course that God has picked out for me, and now I have finished my course. Many others have run the course before me. Since I am encompassed about with so many witnesses, I have laid aside every weight and every besetting sin and have run the race with patience." We can almost see Paul straining every nerve as he runs the race for Jesus. As he comes near the end of his life, he says, "It is all over now. I have triumphed at last because my Lord ran at my side."

God has a course for you to run, also, and you ought to say, "Lord, what do You want me to do? I will be what You want me to be, I'll do what You want me to do, I'll go where You want me to go, if You will only go with me." We do not always choose our course. I did not choose the ministry; God chose me. I had never thought of preaching, but God laid His hand on me and said, "I want you to preach." I answered, "Lord, how can I do it? I have a family, I have no education, I have no money." Then He said, "Leave that up Me." And I did just that, and He brought me through. I met discouragements on every hand, but I could always say in my heart, "God has called me and I must preach." Yes, God says, "Here is the course I want you to take," and you and I will never make much of a contribution to the world if we do not walk in His way.

Some years ago the New York Fire Department had a great parade. One feature of the parade was three busses loaded with people from all walks of life, from a judge to a little boy from the slums. Copies of this sign were on the busses: "All of these were saved by our Fire Department from Burning Buildings." In like manner, as Paul looks back over his course, he sees multitudes who have been saved from sin and death because of the work he has done for Christ. When you come to the end of the way, will anyone be able to say, "I am a Christian because of you"? Will you have any trophies to lay at His feet?

Paul next says, "I have kept the faith." The Lord personally entrusted him with the great gospel truths, and Paul not only preached them, but he lived them out in his life and wrote them out for us in his New Testament letters. Christianity owes more to Paul for preserving these truths than to any other man.

A few years ago two ammunition ships exploded off the coast of California. The little town of Port Chicago was practically ruined. More than three hundred men died in ten seconds time. The flames shot two miles up into the air. The windows in San Francisco, thirty miles away, were broken. But facing the water was a hall in which some people had been holding revival services. On this building was an electric sign, "Jesus Saves." The hall was badly damaged, but the sign still worked and sent its lighted message out over the ruins of the explosion. The world may tumble down around us, but this great truth still remains, "Jesus Saves." This is the faith that Paul kept.

III. How THE OLD SOLDIER FELT ABOUT DEATH

Paul knew that his time had come. He had probably been sentenced to die. This was the last letter that he ever wrote. He tells us: "I am ready to be offered." He is not going to die a natural death; he is going to be slain. As a lamb or an ox is offered up on the sacrificial altar, so is he going to be offered up. "The time of my departure is at hand." He is using a nautical term here. It is time to hoist the anchor and to move out over the ocean. But listen: when a ship sails out of one harbor, we expect it to anchor soon in another harbor. Paul knows that when he moves out of this life, he will cross the ocean of death and anchor his soul forever in the holy city of God.

Now what did he say about death? In Philippians 1:23 he said: "I am in a strait betwixt two, having a desire to depart, and to be with Christ; which is far better: nevertheless to abide in the flesh is more needful for you." He knew that he would be far better off in heaven than on earth, but he said, "It will not be time for me to go up there until I have finished my work down here."

Sometimes in the midst of all the toil and turmoil and strife of this world we get homesick for heaven. We would like to lay every burden down and go on home. But God knows what is best. We are to keep on. We are to do the best we can, and in His own good time He will take us home.

In II Corinthians 5:1 Paul said, "For we know that if our earthly house of this tabernacle were dissolved, we have a building of God, a house not made with hands, eternal in the heavens." He likens the body to a tent and says that some day the tent will fall apart. But when it does God will clothe us with a heavenly body. That body will be eternal. It will never be sick, it will never know pain, it will never get tired. It will be a glorified body, like unto that of the Lord Jesus.

In II Corinthians 5:6-8 Paul told us that while we are here in the body, we are absent from the Lord; but that when we are absent from the body, we are present with the Lord. I stand by the casket of a Christian and I look down at the body, the fleshly thing. I ask the question, "Where is the real person?" And the answer comes back, "He is present with the Lord." When we know that our loved ones are present with Him, we know that they are a thousand times better off than they could ever be in this world. We can weep for ourselves, but we need not weep for our loved ones who die in the Lord.

In I Corinthians 15:19 Paul said, "If in this life only we have hope in Christ, we are of all men most miserable." Hope is the greatest thing in the world. The most miserable people are those who have no hope for the life to come. What does the unsaved man have to look forward to? He can enjoy the pleasures of sin for a season, then death comes. He takes a fearful leap into the dark, and he spends eternity in hell. The sinner boastingly says, "I am not afraid of death," but he does not realize all that it means. The Christian can humbly say, "I have hope in death," for he knows what it will bring to him.

In Philippians 1:21 Paul said, "For me to live is Christ, and to die is gain." Do we gain anything when we die? Do we not lose our loved ones, our friends, our money, our home, everything? Ah, friends, if you can say, "I have lived for Christ," you will gain everything when you die.

You will gain freedom when you die. Freedom from all the aches and pains and sorrows and troubles of life. You will gain fellowship when you die. Our loved ones are going down the valley one by one. But they are waiting for us, and someday we will go out to enjoy fellowship that will never be broken up. But our sweetest fellowship will be the fellowship with Jesus. Paul saw Him on the Damascus road. He never forgot that sight, and he always wanted to see His face again. If you and I have seen Jesus as he did, nothing can keep us from wanting to see His face again. We gain fullness of knowledge if we die in Christ. "Now we see through a glass darkly, but then face to face." We wonder why a wicked person prospers and we have such a hard time. We wonder why a good useful person is taken out of the world and a sorry person is left behind. We wonder why sin comes to break our hearts and blast our hopes and ruin our homes. We will never know in this world, but in the golden glow of that better land we shall sit down by the side of the Lord Jesus and He will explain it all to us. Then we shall understand. Then we shall see that these things which seem so hard to us were simply blessings in disguise.

We gain a home when we die in Christ. It would be wonderful for someone to give us a little home in this world, but we have something better waiting for us in the world to come.

> A tent or a cottage, why should I care?
> They're building a palace for me over there.
> Though exiled from home, yet still may I sing,
> All glory to God, I'm a child of the King.

IV. THE CROWN AWAITING THE OLD SOLDIER

One day they led Paul out to the place of death. He saw the block where his head would lie. He saw the executioner waiting to do his duty. He saw the axe shining in the sun. But he looked beyond all of this and he saw Jesus waiting for him with something in His hand. What was it? Listen: "Henceforth there is laid up for me a crown of righteousness, which the Lord, the righteous judge, shall give me at that day." Forgotten now are all the hardships endured for Christ. Forgotten are the stripes, forgotten are the days and nights in prison, forgotten are the shipwrecks, forgotten are the abuses, forgotten are all the tears that he shed and all the blood that he poured out. This makes up for it all. Christ is waiting to welcome him. The crown is waiting for him. Heaven is waiting for the old soldier.

Are you having a hard time, my friend? Is your body afflicted? Have your friends forsaken you? Do you face many difficulties? Do you have financial worries? Then just keep on. Trust the Lord; do the best you can. He will see you through and bring you home at last.

Paul did not say that this crown was exclusively for him. He said, "Not to me only, but unto all them also that love his appearing." Surely if we love Him and trust Him, we will want to see Him; we will love His appearing. All right, the crown is waiting for you. Some day you will do your last day's work. Some day you will have your last night's sleep. Some day you will endure the last pain and face the last disappointment. Then your soul will soar upward and Jesus will be waiting at the gates. Then He will say, "Come in, I have been waiting for you."

Will it not be awful for anyone, having gone through this life and left Christ out, to miss all of this? But no man needs miss it. Christ says, "Leave your sin, put your trust in Me, and I will make you a child of God and you will have a heavenly home waiting for you at the end of the trail." Is it not wonderful that the way is open to everyone of us? "The gift of God is eternal life through Jesus Christ our Lord." God is not selling anything; He is giving eternal life to all who come unto Him by Christ. Heaven is the only thing that can be had for the asking.

A little girl was lost on the streets of the great city of London. The police found her and tried to help her, but she could not remember her address. "Do you live near Westminster?" they asked her. But she did not recognize that name. "Do you live near the House of Parliament?" "No." "Do you live near Nelson's Statue?" She knew nothing about that. Finally they thought of Charing Cross, where the great stone cross stands. "Do you live near the great cross, my child?" The little tear-stained face lighted up and she said, "O, yes, take me to the Cross. I can get home from there."

Oh, my friends, uncertain, unsettled, unhappy, unsaved, you can get home from the Cross. Do you want to go some day to this wonderful home on high? Then I invite you to the

Cross of Christ. Come and lay all of your burdens down. Come and let Him take you in His arms and forgive you and save you. Then at the end of the way you, too, will be able to say, " 'I have fought a good fight, I have finished my course, I have kept the faith: henceforth there is laid up for me a crown of righteousness,' and I am going home to be with Jesus forever."

5

But There Is a God in Heaven

But there is a God in heaven . . . (Dan. 2:28).

Nebuchadnezzar was the king of Babylon. One night he had a dream that troubled him greatly. Sleep fled from his eyes. In the early morning his dream still lingered with him. He was greatly puzzled. He called all of his wise men and magicians together and said to them, "Tell me the meaning of my dream." They replied, "We will try to do that if you will tell us the dream." And the king said, "I have forgotten the dream, but you claim to be wise men and great men, surely you can tell me what I dreamed and you can tell me the meaning thereof. If you cannot do this, I will have you cut to pieces." "We will try," said the wise men, "but give us time." They put their heads together and tried to find a solution for the problem, but they were helpless.

In the city of Babylon, however, there happened to be a young man who was a true friend of God. This young man was Daniel. He went before the king and said, "Give me just a little time and I will tell you the dream and the interpretation thereof." Then he did a fine thing. He went home and called three of his friends together and said to them, "I want you to pray with me and ask God to reveal to me the dream and the interpretation." In the middle of the night, after they had prayed long and earnestly, the vision came and it was entirely clear to Daniel. Then Daniel did another fine thing. He went down upon his knees and thanked God for revealing the truth to him.

The next day Daniel went before the king and said to him, "There isn't a man upon the earth who could tell you your dream and the interpretation of it, 'but there is a God in heaven' and He has revealed the dream to me." He then told the king the dream and the meaning thereof. This pleased the king so much that he gave Daniel many rich gifts and made him ruler over Babylon and chief over his wise men.

You and I, in every hour of trouble, can say, "'But there is a God in heaven.' These things are hard, 'but there is a God in heaven' and He will help and deliver me." Even in the midst of war and bloodshed, when our homes and hearts are being broken, we can remember that there is a God in heaven and that He will cause all things to work out for our good and His great glory.

I. Moses Learned This Great Truth at the Red Sea

For many years the children of Israel had been in bondage. Then one day God said, "They have had enough." He called Moses and sent him down into Egypt. Moses appeared before the king of Egypt and gave him the message of the Lord, "Let my people go." Then followed many trials and disappointments, but at last they were on the way out. Thousands and thousands of God's people marched out of Egypt. The king allowed them to go, and they went happily on their way toward the Promised Land.

One day they came to the shores of the mighty Red Sea and it lay before them forbidding and impassable. They looked back and saw clouds of dust. The soldiers of Pharaoh were coming after them and their swords could be seen glistening in the sun. The people knew that they would be drowned or killed or taken back to become slaves of Egypt. They were helpless and hopeless: in front of them the sea, on either side the mountains and in back the hosts of Pharaoh. The scared people cried out to Moses, "Why did you bring us here to die? Were there no graves in Egypt? It would have been better for us to serve always as slaves than to die in the wilderness." Moses replied, "Pharaoh is a great king; his army is mighty and the sea is wide; 'but there is a God in heaven' and He will deliver us."

Then Moses cried out unto God, and the Lord spoke unto him saying, "Speak unto the children of Israel and tell them to go forward. Lift up your rod over the sea and I will permit you to go across on dry land. Then watch and see what happens to the Egyptians." Moses lifted up his rod, and soon there was a dry path through the middle of the waters, which were backed up like walls on either side. Israel marched through and landed safely on the other shore. The Egyptians said, "If the Israelites can do that, we can do it, too." But God caused the waters to roll over them, and they were drowned in the midst of the sea.

Listen! What is that sound on the other shore? It is not murmuring; it is not grumbling; it is a song of praise to God. And what is the burden of their song? They are saying, "Man may be mighty and he may try to hold us, 'but there is a God in heaven' and He will deliver us if we trust Him." Hundreds of years pass by and every time the Israelites talk and sing about the greatness of God, they talk and sing about how He delivered their forefathers at the Red Sea.

Have there been times of great distress for you? Have you been bound in on every side, knowing not which way to go? Has your pathway been full of dangers? Oh, just remember that there is a God in heaven! Pour out your soul to Him, and He will open up the way and lead you into life and joy.

II. Shadrach, Meshach and Abed-nego Learned This Truth in the Fiery Furnace

At one point during his reign King Nebuchadnezzar built an image of gold and set it in the midst of the plains. It was an imposing statue, ninety-five feet high. The king then sent a decree out from the palace: "Let all the people bow down and worship this image, or they will be thrown into the fiery furnace." Everyone in the land came and, falling upon their knees, they worshiped the golden image. But there were three young Hebrews who refused to bow down. Shadrach, Meshach and Abed-nego bowed before no one except the God of heaven. In his fury the king sent for them and said to them, "Why did you not bow down before the golden image?" And they replied, "There is just one God. 'There is a God in heaven,' and we shall bow down to none except to Him. If you put us in the fiery furnace, we believe He will deliver us; but even if He does not, we shall still bow down to no other god."

The more these young men talked, the more angry became the king. He sent out orders to his servants: "Heat the furnace seven times hotter than ever and bind these young men and throw them into the fire." The servants grasped the young men and bound them. What an awful thing for Shadrach, Meshach and Abed-nego — "but there is a God in heaven." They were thrown into the fiery furnace, but the fire did not hurt them. The only thing it could do was to burn off their bonds and set them free. The king came down and looked into the furnace and said, "Three men were thrown into the furnace, but I see four of them and the fourth is like unto the Son of God." Then he called the men out of the fiery furnace and was obliged to say, "There is indeed a God in heaven!"

There may come a time when you are forced to take a stand either for or against God. It may mean persecution for you, but remember, "there is a God in heaven." There may come a time when you are thrown into the fiery furnace of suffering and affliction; but when that time comes just remember, 'there is a God in heaven." He is bigger than anyone else; He has more power than all the others. Trust in Him and He will bring you out safely.

III. DANIEL LEARNED THIS TRUTH
IN THE LION'S DEN

You know the old story. A decree was sent out saying that no one should be worshiped but the king. But Daniel, God's man, paid no more attention to this decree than he did to a passing breeze. Three times daily he knelt before his window and offered his prayer to God. Because of his disobedience to the laws, the order was soon given that Daniel was to be thrown into the lion's den. Poor old Daniel! Maybe he should have drawn the shades so that his enemies could not see him praying. But not this man — he is the most courageous man of the Old Testament. Down in his heart there was a song and this was it, "There is a God in heaven."

Before Daniel reached the lion's den, God went to work. He touched the lion's head and said, "One of my servants is coming to spend the night here. Be nice to him; let him sleep well; make him comfortable; lend your shaggy mane as a pillow for him and do not harm a hair of his head." And it seems that the lions nod their heads in obedient assent. In a minute the iron door is opened and Daniel drops down into the den. The lions welcome him. He lies down and goes to sleep like a baby, while they watch over him through the night.

The next morning King Darius came down into the den and said, "O Daniel, are you safe?" And Daniel answered, "O king, there is a God in heaven. He took care of me and gave me a good night's rest. And how are you this morning?"

Oh, my friends, stand up for God. Though you be cast into the den of lions, "there is a God in heaven" and He will take care of you.

IV. PETER LEARNED THIS TRUTH IN THE PRISON CELL

Peter and the other apostles were preaching the Gospel. Herod, the chief politician, wanted to sway the people in his own favor. He had killed James with the sword and when he saw how it pleased the people, he cast Peter into prison. "I have him now," says Herod. "I will kill him tomorrow." "We have him now," say the Jews. "This fellow will not trouble us any more." "But there is a God in heaven," and Peter knew this God. So he lay down and went to sleep, chained to guards on either side. He was the only Christian asleep in Jerusalem that night. All the others were praying for his deliverance. God in heaven heard the prayers and an angel came into the prison, released Peter and restored him to the praying church.

Herod, you may persecute the preacher if you want to, you may kill James and imprison Peter — that is your privilege — but remember, "there is a God in heaven," and He has said, "Touch not mine anointed." Now what happens to Mr. Herod? Just read the next verse in this chapter. He sat upon his throne and made a speech to the people. They applauded him greatly, saying, "It is the voice of a god." Suddenly the angel of the Lord struck the king and he toppled from his throne, a dead man. And we read, "He was eaten of worms and gave up the ghost." Be careful how you treat God's servants, for there is still a God in heaven.

V. Remember When You Have Sinned That There is a God in Heaven

There are so many things to remember in this connection. First, God knows about your sin. You look north and south, east and west and no one is the witness to your sin. But God is looking on. God knows about it whether it is committed in the brightness of the midday sun or in the blackness of the midnight hour.

In my boyhood home there was a certain picture with an eye at the top of it. The eye represented the all-seeing eye of God. This eye looked down upon everything in the whole picture. So God looks down upon everything in the picture of our lives. He sees the sparrow when it falls; He watches the lily as it grows in the field; He looks upon every star that twinkles in the heavens; He sees every sin that we commit.

The second thing to remember is that God is quick to forgive us if we confess our sins. For we read, "If we confess our sins, he is faithful and just to forgive us our sins and to cleanse us from all unrighteousness." Yes, all of us have sinned; but we are not beyond hope if we fall before Him, confess our sins and ask His forgiveness. He does not hesitate; forgiveness is ours in that instant .

Yonder is the prodigal son coming home. He knows that he has sinned; he feels the burden of it in his heart. He sees his father and cries out, "I have sinned, and am no more worthy to be called thy son." But the father cuts off his confession; he does not let the boy say a word about his sin. He just wraps his loving arms around him and forgives him and says to the servants, "Bring out the best that we have. My boy has come home." That is the way God does when we come confessing our sins to Him. Yes, when you have sinned, remember that "there is a God in heaven"; remember that He knows about your sins and that when you confess them unto Him, He is quick to forgive.

VI. REMEMBER IN THE TIME OF TROUBLE AND SORROW THAT THERE IS A GOD IN HEAVEN

There are many hours when God seems especially close to us. He seems close in some great religious service. He seems close when we stand and look at the glow of the sunset in the West. He seems close when He opens up His storehouse and pours out a great blessing. But surely God is closer in the time of trouble and sorrow than at other times. I hear people say, "If such and such a thing should happen to me, I could not stand it." That very thing may come to you someday and then will be the time to say: "There is a God in heaven."

I went to the Bible to find a few Scriptures on God's comfort. I found one hundred and twenty-five great comforting texts, but I believe the finest and sweetest one is in Matthew 11:28, where Jesus said, "Come unto me, all ye that labour and are heavy laden, and I will give you rest." Yes, in sorrow and trouble remember that there is a God in heaven. He is always loving and compassionate and He will give you comfort and grace.

VII. REMEMBER THAT THERE WILL BE A GOD IN HEAVEN WHEN YOU GET TO THE END OF THE WAY

One day Old Death will come knocking at the door. You will not be able to keep the door locked, and he will come in. The Devil may speak up and say, "I want this soul for my abode." "But there is a God in heaven," and He will say, "This soul is mine; I have redeemed him; He believed on My Son and he is safe now and forevermore."

There is no maybe about it, my friend. "He that believeth on the Son hath eternal life" (John 3:36). "There is . . .

no condemnation to them which are in Christ Jesus" (Rom. 8:1). "No man is able to pluck them out of my Father's hand" (John 10:29). "He that doeth the will of God abideth for ever" (I John 2:17).

Yes, my friend, if Christ is yours you need have no fear of death. "There is a God in heaven," and He will carry you safely through and bring you to the home on the other shore.

One day in Rome soldiers led Paul out into the public square. The execution block was ready; the soldier's axe was sharp. "Paul, do you have anything to say?" I can hear Paul saying, " 'I know whom I have believed, and am persuaded that he is able to keep that which I have committed unto him against that day.' 'For me to live is Christ, and to die is gain.' May God bless and forgive you all." His head is laid on the block; the axe glistens in the sun for a moment and then comes down upon the apostle's neck. Paul is gone now, "but there is a God in heaven." Paul's head rolls off the block, but his soul goes to be with Christ forevermore.

Do you know and love and trust the Saviour whom Paul served? If you do, you need never fear. "There is a God in heaven," and you are His. He will watch over you and care for you and take you home safely at last.

6

Barriers to Blessing

And when they could not come nigh unto him for the press, they uncovered the roof where he was: and when they had broken it up, they let down the bed whereon the sick of the palsy lay (Mark 2:4).

When I was a schoolboy, I read the old story about the dykes of Holland. According to the story, one day one of the dykes sprang a leak and the water began pouring in through a certain hole. But a heroic boy thrust his arm into the hole and held the waters back and saved the city from possible destruction. I am afraid that you and I have held back some waters too—the waters of blessing. God has wanted to bless us, but our lives have not been what they should have been and we have held back the blessing. He has wanted to bless other lives through us and we have held back His blessing from them, too.

In the text we see Jesus preaching in a certain house. A crowd had gathered, a crowd that filled the whole house and overflowed into the courtyard. Every door was blocked by a mass of humanity. Down the street lay a sick man. Although he was a sick man he was a fortunate man, for he had four friends who wanted to bring him to Jesus. His friends went down to get him, but they could not bring him into the presence of Jesus because of the crowd. This crowd erected a

barrier between the man and the blessing that Jesus had for
him. You remember how the friends took him up on the
roof and let him down into the healing, forgiving presence of
the Saviour. We, too, have been barriers to blessing. If we
are not living as we ought to live, if our hearts are not right
in God's sight, we erect barriers that keep blessings from us
and from others.

The Christian life is a thing of the spirit. It is the spirit that
you have that really counts. If we have the wrong spirit, blessings can never flow to us or through us. Let us look at some
of these spirits.

I. A Covetous Spirit is a Barrier to Blessing

Achan is an illustration of this spirit. He coveted the forbidden things in the city of Jericho, and because of this
covetousness he brought defeat to Joshua's army and death
to himself and family. God would have blessed Achan and his
family, but Achan cut off the blessing by his covetousness.

God says, "Will a man rob God? Yet ye have robbed me"
(Mal. 3:8). And then He tells how the blessings are cut off
because of our covetousness. When God commands anything
He attaches a promise everytime. He commands us to tithe
and then says, "I will open you up the windows of heaven,
and pour you out a blessing" (Mal. 3:10). There is a real
blessing for the tither. If you love money and keep it
and spend it for yourself, if you keep that from God which
belongs to Him, you are surely erecting a barrier. Why not try
God's plan? Why not launch out upon His promises and give
Him a chance to bless you? He cannot bless you as long
as you erect a barrier by your own covetousness.

One of the Ten Commandments reads, "Thou shalt not
covet." Sometimes we look out and see others enjoying the
things which we do not have, and immediately something

rises within us, something terrible and hurtful — the spirit of covetousness. We ought immediately to kill that spirit as we would a rattlesnake, for covetousness cuts off the blessings of God.

II. A Rebellious Spirit is a Barrier To Blessing

Take the case of Jonah. God wanted to bless him and make him a blessing to the people of Ninevah. To this preacher He said one word, "Go." That is a small word, but it carries a big blessing with it. But the preacher said to God, "No." That is a small word, too, but it cuts off the blessing. There came a time when God conquered Jonah's rebellious spirit, but the Lord had to send Jonah through much trouble before the preacher learned his lesson.

I have seen people rebel against God. A loved one dies; they do not think it is right; and they cry out, "He shouldn't have been taken away from me!" Or they have a hard time and they say, "Why has this happened to me?" God is blamed for all of their trouble. With their rebellious spirit they build a wall, and no blessings can get over it. God has a plan for your life, but if you rebel against that plan you cannot expect the blessings of God.

III. A Worldly Spirit is a Barrier to Blessing

Demas is an illustration of this point. He was a young man who heard Paul preach one day. He was charmed by the personality of the preacher. Every word was a challenge to his heart. In a great moment of spiritual ecstasy he cried out, "I will leave everything and go with this man in the service of Jesus Christ." Wasn't that fine? There is nothing more romantic than a young man adventuring for Christ. Demas started out in a fine way. He was right by Paul's side. He was a joy and a help to him. But they journeyed to the great city, and the bright lights of the world blinded the eyes of Demas. And then we read these sad words spoken by Paul: "Demas hath forsaken me, having loved this present world" (II Tim. 4:10). Thus Demas cut off every blessing for himself and for others whom he might have served.

Oh, there are so many like Demas in the world! They start out for Christ in a wonderful way, and then one day the world calls to them. They listen; they follow. From that moment Christ and the Church have no room in their lives. The blessings cease to come to them and through them.

Many of you in your social life have friends whom you could help toward Christ and the Church and heaven, but you do the worldly things which they do and you have no influence over them. God wants you to be a channel through which His blessings go flowing to these friends, but instead you have become a barrier because of your worldly spirit.

A man bought a sub-division and went out to develop it. Said he to his pastor, "Pastor, I will not be at church for a while, but when I have sold these lots I will come back. He soon had sold the lots, but he did not come back. Such a person hardly ever does come back. When the spirit of the world gets hold of a man it always takes him down.

IV. A Prayerless Spirit is a Barrier to Blessing

James says, "Ye have not, because ye ask not" (James 4:2). He is telling us that God wants us to have the blessings, but that we choke the channels when we neglect to pray. Sometime ago a young man was starving in an attic, although his father was a rich man. When the father was notified he said, "Oh, if I had only known! If he had only called upon me, I would have given him anything I have." How foolish it was for the man to starve simply because he refused to ask. God

has all that we need. If we do not get all that we need, it is
because we are not asking for it.

> Oh, what peace we often forfeit,
> Oh, what needless pain we bear —
> All because we do not carry
> Everything to God in prayer.

John Knox of Scotland invited some friends to his house
to meet a group of people. After a time they missed their
host. After a search they found him in the garden, his face
was buried in his hands and in deep agony he was crying,
"O God, give me Scotland or I die!" God did something
through him. Scotland never lost the definite spiritual im-
pact that came to her through John Knox. God can use us, too,
if we will but pray.

V. An Unforgiving Spirit is a Barrier to Blessing

Jesus had the right spirit. It is Friday — black Friday —
a crowd journeys out from the city of Jerusalem, down the
Via Dolorosa and to a place called Calvary. Soon three crosses
are outlined against the sky. On these three crosses three
men are dying in agony and blood. The crowd is taunting
and jeering these men. From the center cross I hear a voice. Is
that Man condemning? Is He cursing? No, He is praying.
Listen to Him, "Father, forgive them; for they know not what
they do" (Luke 23:34).

What? Did we hear Him aright? Yes, that was His prayer.
He had the right spirit. Though they were killing Him, He
asked forgiveness for them. Hear me, my friends. If you do
not have this same spirit, you are not following Jesus, and the
blessings of God cannot flow to you nor through you.

Some years ago I was holding a meeting in South Carolina.
Two men in the church, a man and his son-in-law, had not
spoken to each other for many years. Each of them came to
church every Sunday. The father-in-law sat on one side of

the church and the son-in-law sat on the other side. One afternoon I preached a sermon which God used to touch their hearts. During the invitation I saw the father-in-law stand on tip-toe and look across the congregation at his son-in-law. I looked over at the son-in-law and he was looking over the heads of the congregation at his father-in-law. In a moment I saw the father-in-law start down the aisle toward the front of the church. In a moment the son-in-law came down the other aisle. When they met in front of the pulpit, they reached out their hands to shake hands with each other, but this never happened. Suddenly their arms were around each other and they were sobbing and loving each other and putting aside all their differences. Believe me, from that moment on the floodtides of revival ran high and many people were saved. The barrier had been removed. There are such tragedies all around us today. You are hindering someone if you have an unforgiving spirit.

VI. A Critical Spirit is a Barrier to Blessing

A learned man said to Mr. Moody one day, "You made thirty-eight grammatical errors in your sermon today." Mr. Moody replied, "I am quite sure that I must have made even more than that. I have not had the educational advantages that you have had, but I am trying to use all that I have for the glory of God, are you?" How much did that man get out of Mr. Moody's sermon? The man who looks for only the mistakes of others finds little in life with which to enrich himself.

Criticism is the poorest substitute in the world for service. I saw a good motto in a store sometime ago; it read like this: "Come in without knocking—go out the same way!" Let us not belong to the "knockers' gang."

In our critical way we often judge men by what we have

seen, when really and truly we do not know their hearts. We throw our selfrighteous robes around us, we flash our critical eyes upon them and say, "Thank God, I am not like these other men." And yet we do not know the things that are deep down in their hearts. In many ways they may be many times finer than we are. A critical spirit is a barrier to blessing. Let us get rid of it.

VII. An Indifferent Spirit is a Barrier to Blessing

Gallio is our illustration here. He was deputy at Corinth, and he had a chance to hear a great man deliver a great message when Paul was brought before him. But we read his character in these words: "Gallio cared for none of those things." (Acts 18:17).

This is true of so many people today. God blesses a church in a wonderful way: souls are being saved and happy fellowship is being enjoyed. "Were you at church yesterday?" you ask someone on Monday. "No, I wasn't there," is the reply, and then you must listen to a long string of excuses. But the sum total of all that is said is this: "I care for none of those things."

The Psalmist said, "I was glad when they said unto me, Let us go into the house of the Lord." (Ps. 122:1). But you say, "I care for none of those things." In Hebrews 10:25 we read, "Forsake not the assembling of yourselves together." But you say, "I care for none of these things."

Our churches have millians of members today, but the majority of them have an indifferent spirit. Yet our communities would not be worth living in if they lost the influence of our churches. Let us be different from Gallio. Let us show that we do have a real concern for the things of God.

VII. A Spirit of Self-glorification is a Barrier to Blessing

There are some people who speak piously of their religion. They tell you how much they love the Lord and His work, but if they can not have a job where they receive most of the glory they immediately resign. Why can we not serve God in a small place? Browning said, "All service ranks the same with God." It would be a poor army if all men were generals; we need some privates. It is even so with the Church. The spirit of self-glorification is indeed a barrier to blessing.

IX. A Disobedient Spirit is a Barrier to Blessing

Look at King Saul. He was chosen by the Lord for a mighty work. He had a great future as the leader of God's people. But there came a time when he disobeyed the voice of God, and God was forced to say to him, "Since you have disobeyed me, I must take the kingdom from you and give it to another." Contrast King Saul to the Apostle Paul. "What would you have me do?" asked Paul. "I will show you how much you must suffer for My Name's sake," replied the Lord. Paul was not disobedient to the heavenly vision, for he tells us later, "I was not disobedient." And because of his obedience the Lord sent blessings through him to multitudes of souls. No wonder he could say at the end of the way, "I have fought a good fight, there is laid up for me a crown of righteousness."

Is God telling you that a certain course is right? In obedience there is a blessing for you and for others. In your disobedience you erect a barrier and cut off blessings that might come to you and them.

Do you have any of these wrong spirits within your heart? If so, you are hurting not only yourself but others. God wants us to be channels, not reservoirs. There are many around us who need His blessings, but if our lives are choked with wrong they will never receive them.

Dr. S. D. Gordon tells this story about a certain city. There was a great reservoir which supplied the city with its water. One day the water supply failed. Men were sent out to investigate, but they could not learn why the water was not flowing into the city. Then they received a letter from a city employee who had been discharged. "In a certain place you will find a plug in the pipe," the letter read, "I placed it there in my anger." The workmen were soon on the job and the plug was pulled out. Then again the fresh sparkling water came rushing down to refresh the city.

O friend, pull the plug out! Take out that old plug of an ugly unchristian spirit. Find the thing that stands between you and God, tear it out by the roots, cast it aside, then the blessings of God will flow into your own life and out to refresh the lives of others.

7

God's "All Things"

And we know that all things work together for good to them that love God, to them who are the called according to his purpose (Rom. 8:28).

One day a man took his little son to the top of a high hill. He pointed in every direction — north, east, south and west. "My boy," he said, "God's love is as big as all that." "Yes, Dad," said the little boy, "and just think, we are right in the middle of it." Oh, yes, God is a great God and His love is a great love — and we are right in the midst of it all!

But here is the trouble in the world today. Men believe in a little God and a big humanity. Man is taking the place of God. With all of man's inventions and progress he feels that he is outgrowing the Lord. Man is being glorified and God is being pushed into the background. In Japan the emperor was once worshiped as a god. The Japanese people knew nothing of the Heavenly Father; they were dependent upon the might of men and arms. In Germany some years ago Hitler was God. Germans bowed down and worshiped him and his way of life, or went the way of thousands who disobeyed him. Yes, man is being glorified and God is forgotten. But my friends, God will not be left out; He *will* make Himself known and felt in the world. He is still a great sovereign God. He made all things, they are His now, and He will finally reign over all things.

I have stood on the top of the highest mountain east of the Mississippi River and have looked many miles in every direction. I have looked through a telescope from the top of Lookout Mountain in Tennessee and was told that I was looking into seven states. As the vision spreads to such a great distance, taking in the majestic mountains and lowly plains, a man feels quite small in the presence of the wonders of God. David must have felt that way when he said, "When I consider thy heavens, the work of thy fingers, the moon and the stars, which thou has ordained; what is man that thou art mindful of him? and the son of man, that thou visiteth him?" (Ps. 8:3, 4).

The subject of this message is "God's 'All Things'." I am thinking of four places in the Bible where these words are used. These four texts cover everything from the creation to God's final victory.

I. The "All Things" of Creation

"All things were made by him; and without him was not any thing made that was made." (John 1:3)

Man can do some wonderful things. He can make a mighty steamer to sail the seas, or a splendid submarine to sail under the seas, or a great airplane to fly above the seas. He can build a skyscraper one hundred and two stories high. He can build a highway from one end of the country to another, with bridges spanning every river and valley. He can build an automobile that will fly down this highway ninety miles per hour. He can build a radio that will reach five thousand miles into the air and pluck from it voices on the other side of the world. He can build a telephone over which he can talk ten thousand miles. Yes, man can build many wonderful things. But this is true of all which he builds: he builds it out of something else, out of pre-existing materials. Not so with God. He created the world and made it all out of nothing. He created it without the aid of any materials. He spoke and it came into being.

He spoke, and there was light in the world. He spoke, and the land was formed. He spoke, and the mountains and rivers and seas came into existence. He spoke, and made the trees and flowers and grass. He spoke, and the sun and moon and stars glittered in the heavens. He spoke, and the world was filled with animals and fowls. He spoke, and the waters were filled with fish. Yes, God has created all things that are in the world. But when He looked on these things, though He saw they were good, He knew that something was missing. So I imagine that God said, "That is not enough. I will now make My masterpiece. I will make man with a wonderful mind and body and soul. I will give him dominion over all things. I will make him in My own image." Then God spoke, and man stood before Him, the masterpiece of His creation.

Think of what a wonderful thing the human body is. A great river of blood runs through the body. Five million little boats called corpuscles work up and down the blood stream to build up the body and carry off the waste. The heart is a wonderful pumping station which works every hour whether we are awake or asleep. It contracts sixty times per minute or thirty-six hundred times per hour. Every time it beats it lifts two ounces of blood. In one hour three hundred and fifty pounds of blood pass through the heart. God was thinking great thoughts when He made man's heart.

Then think of the wonders of the human ear. Think of the hammer and anvil and the stirrup and the delicate strings. Think of the mysterious passages which carry sound to the brain. Think of the wonders of the human eye. The eye picks up an object, turns it about, throws it upon the screen of the brain and you see it as a true picture. Oh, we could go on thus for hours about the wonders of a God-created man!

God created Niagara Falls and its millions of gallons of water pouring over a mighty precipice every minute. He created the wonderful caverns with their mysterious display of stalactites and stalagmites, which require one hundred years for an inch of growth. He created the Grand Canyon of the Colorado. He created all the wonders of the land and sea and sky. The rising sun is the creation of His great hand. The wonderful colors of the West in the evening are evidence of His eye for beauty. Wonders everywhere, beauty everywhere, wonderful workings of nature everywhere. Sunshine, rain, sleet, snow, water and waves — God created all of these things. What a mighty God He is! "Without him was not any thing made that was made."

II. The "All Things" of Regeneration

"Therefore if any man be in Christ, he is a new creature: old things are passed away; behold, all things are become new" (II Cor. 5:17)

God made all things good. Moreover he made man without sin. But man did not remain in that condition. He disobeyed God, he broke His laws and in sin he dragged the human race downward. But God made provisions for man to climb out of the darkness of sin. Nineteen hundred years ago God made the ladder, building it out of His Only-begotten Son. Now He tells the sinful man to come to Him and promises to make him an absolutely new man, all changed on the inside. Man often changes when he becomes wealthy, when he gets married, when he gets a new job, when he has an added responsibility, when he comes to old age. But there is no change in all the world so radical as that change which comes to the sinner when he comes to Jesus.

1. *He has a new life.* No longer does he live upon the low level of sin; he lives the higher life. Florence Nightingale once said to a doctor, "How do you treat pneumonia?" The doctor answered, "We do not treat pneumonia; we treat the patient." The world is full of the disease of sin, but Jesus does not treat the disease; He treats the patient. He makes the heart of the patient over and the redeemed man lives a new life.

2. *He has a new loyalty.* No longer is he loyal to evil, but to the higher things. No longer does he frequent the places of sin. His feet find their way to the Father's house. He has a higher and greater loyalty than ever.

3. *He has a new love.* Once he loved the things of Satan and hated the things of God, but now he loves the things of God and hates the things of Satan. We have seen that happen often. Here is a man who could not be dragged into the church. He had absolutely nothing to do with spiritual things. But one day the Lord gets hold of his heart. He is born again and now looks forward to every meeting in God's house.

4. *He has new longings.* All of his dreams and ambitions are changed. He longs to please Christ and not the world. He longs to serve Him and honor Him. He longs to live a good life so that he will not be ashamed at His coming. He longs to meet Him face to face and hear Him say, "Well done thou good and faithful servant."

In the great fire of London St. Paul's Cathedral was destroyed. The queen called upon Sir Christopher Wren to rebuild the Cathedral. He decided to erect the grandest place of worship in the kingdom. When he viewed the ruins however, he found that not one piece of the old cathedral could be used. So he carried away all the rubbish and built anew. So it is with us. Christ looks into our lives and finds there all the rubbish of sin and folly. But He removes all this, He lays the foundation in His own blood and He builds a new structure which is called "the new man." So it is that all things become new in the presence of regeneration.

III. The "All Things" Working Together

"And we know that all things work together for good to them that love God, to them who are the called according to his purpose." (Rom. 8:28)

This is one of the most blessed promises in the Bible, but men do not believe it. They do not believe that God is behind everything, working it out for our good. They have a hard time, they cannot understand why the troubles come their way. But they need to look up into the light out of darkness and say, "I know not why this has come, I know not what is coming tomorrow, but I know it will work out for my good."

The text does not say that all things will work out for good to all people. Only to those who love God do all things work together for good. The promise is to His own children and not to anyone else. If a man is living in sin he cannot say, "These things are being worked out by the Lord for my good." They do not work together for good unless you are loving God and living for Him.

The Christian can stand at a casket and say good-bye to the dearest on earth to him and know that these words are true. In his hour of deepest sorrow and hardest trial and greatest temptation, he can know they are true. Though he faces the hardest things in life, he knows that these things cannot change the eternal Word of God.

The text says "all things" and not just some things. Not merely the pleasant things and the easy things, but all things.

We see the good things working together for us, but let me tell you that the bad things work around for our good also. We cannot see this while they are happening, but some day we will see it. Mystery may engulf you and enemies may assail you and friends may desert you; Satan may buffet you and demons beset you; sins may infest you and sickness weaken you; sorrows may distress you and death rob you and poverty threaten you; air castles may crumble at your feet; your dreams may vanish and your ships may go on the reef; the raging storm may sweep down upon you and dark clouds may swallow you; but still all things work together for good to them that love God.

Notice that all things work together for good now — this is present tense. You say, "I cannot see any good in this thing," but that is no sign that God is not working. When the darkest hours come and the demons of hell are around you, you feel that God has hidden His face. But even then He is still busy, and after a while the sun will rise for you and you will see that God's loving hand was in it all the time.

Notice that these things work together — not separately, nor individually, but together. God did not say that all things are good, but that they all work together for good. Many people pick out one experience and wave it in God's face and say "There is no good in that thing." But He says that when all things work together it is part of the Divine plan. It takes all the experiences of life to make the whole. Everything has a definite place; and when these things go to work together, the result is that it all comes out for our good.

A diamond must be cut to bring out its beauty; gold must be refined to bring out its purity; the vine must be pruned to bear fruit; the clay must be molded to make it a fit vessel. So must the child of God be cut and refined and pruned and molded to fit him for the Master's use. The process seems hard, but we ought always to sing:

Have Thine own way, Lord! Have Thine own way!
Thou art the Potter; I am the clay.
Mold me and make me after Thy will,
While I am waiting, yielded and still.

Today this old world is in a seething turmoil. Well, my friends, the collective troubles of the world will work together for the Christian's good. God will work it out all right. It may mean the taking of some of us out of the world and into heaven, but that will still be well. At the bottom of every page of history there should be written these words: "God reigns."

Let us not be in despair over the conditions of the world. We are to be concerned, of course; our hearts will be going out to all who suffer. But in the midst of it all let us have a quiet faith which is rooted deeply in the goodness of God. As our daily portion let us remember "that all things work together for good to them that love God."

IV. The "All Things" of Christ's Pre-eminence

"That in all things he might have the pre-eminence." (Col. 1:18)

There have been some great men in the eyes of the world. They came, they saw, they conquered, and they died. But there has never been one like Jesus.

He came into the world, He walked among men, He died, He conquered death and the grave, and He rose again. Now He stands as the highest figure in the universe — pre-eminent in all things.

1. *He is pre-eminent in history.* History is simply "His story." There have been times in the world's history when it seemed that civilization was tottering on the brink. It seemed that God was dead and that evil had the upper hand.

But in the dim shadow there stood the everlasting Christ, watching over His own. He would let the world go so far, then He would reach forth His hand, call a halt and set things right. He is pre-eminent in history.

2. *He is pre-eminent in the Bible.* Why do we have the Bible? It is given to us simply to reveal Christ and His wondrous works. Every book from Genesis to Revelation, is a biography of Jesus. Martin Luther said, "There is but one Book and one Person. The book is the Bible and the person is Christ." This Book exhibits and exalts the Saviour.

3. *He is pre-eminent in nature.* "The heavens declare the glory of God." He is the creator and sustainer of all the rolling spheres. Creation is His child. The seasons revolve around the calendar year because they are held in His hand. The sun and the moon and the stars take their rightful place in the sky and perform their given tasks because He is running the universe.

4. *He is pre-eminent in prophecy.* The Book of God tells us of the moving events that will come at the end of this present age. The greatest actor in the final drama will be Jesus. He will come from heaven with a shout and He will gather all of his loved ones, dead and alive, and take them home to glory with Him. He will stay there for a time and then He will lead all of His saints out of heaven and come sweeping down the expanse of the skies. He will chain the Devil and reign upon the earth for a thousand years. Then He will bring all these things to an end. He will cast Satan and his wicked ones into the Lake of Fire and give us a home forever in the Heavenly City.

He is the center of all that is going to happen. Until He comes none of these things can happen. When we look at the world today we see how it does need the touch of His mighty hand; things will never change until He comes. It may be that things are shaping up for His coming now. Are you ready for that time? Can you say, "Lord, if this is the time, I am ready"? Yes, my friends, Christ is pre-eminent. Is he pre-eminent in your life? Have you given your heart to Him? Are you keeping that heart clean for Him? Are you giving Him first place in your life? Is there anything beween you and Him today?

One day a North Carolina farmer drove two high-spirited horses into town. He left the horses at the hitching post and went into the store. While he was gone the horses became frightened, broke away and started running down the street. Just then the man came out of the store, ran out into the street and seized the reins. Finally the horses stopped, reared into the air and came down with their hoofs on the body of the man. Someone finally pulled the man from under the horses. He was in the last agony of death. They said to him, "Why did you sacrifice your life just for the horses and the wagon?" And the man replied, as he breathed his last breath, "Go look in the wagon — go look in the wagon!" And in the straw they found a little boy fast asleep. Then no one said that the sacrifice was too great.

Oh, my friends, there was One who knew we were on the way to death! He dashed out and went to the Cross and there gave His life for you and me. He makes us all that we are today; He gives us all the hope that we have for tomorrow. He is the pre-eminent Saviour. Is He your Saviour? Does He have first place in your heart?

8

There'll Be Some Changes Made

> Behold, I show you a mystery; We shall not all sleep, but we shall all be changed, in a moment, in the twinkling of an eye, at the last trump: for the trumpet shall sound, and the dead shall be raised incorruptible, and we shall be changed (I Cor. 15:51-52).

We are certainly living in a changing world. There is only one human thing certain in this old world and that is the fact of change. There is nothing so certain and sure as change. We do not know what changes are coming, but we are sure that they will come.

Places change. The dusty road that used to run by the home of my father is now a ribbon of concrete. The field in which I picked cotton is now a community of lovely homes. We talk to a friend about a city which they have not visited for fifteen or twenty years and we say, "You would not know the place now." Many of our cities and towns were almost dead a few years ago. Stores were vacant and many houses were empty, but those cities are booming now and it is almost impossible to find a place to live. Yes, places change.

People change. The girl who once was an ugly duckling became a ravishing beauty and won a beauty contest. I once knew a boy who could never behave in church. He brought trouble to his teachers and leaders who worked with him. But people change, you know, and he is now a splendid preacher of the Gospel. Money may change a man — a

83

man inherits a fortune, passes his old friends by and forgets the old neighborhood. Illness may change a strong and vigorous person into an invalid. Yes, people change.

Customs change also. Once we rode in oxcarts, but today we fly all over the world in speedy planes. Our mail was once carried by the pony express, but today air mail speeds it across the continent in a short time. Today we have the cable, the radio, the television and the telephone. Surgeons used to bleed their patients for a certain disease, later on they boiled them, and now they freeze them for the same disease. Customs are changing every day.

Yes, this world is full of changes. Natural changes are going on all around us, but today I want to tell you of some spiritual changes.

I. There is the Change Created by the New Birth

"Therefore if any man be in Christ, he is a new creature: old things are passed away; behold, all things are become new" (II Cor. 5:17).

In the old days the evangelist would come to town and he would advertise that on a certain night he would tell the story of his life. His theme would be, "From the Gambling Hall to the Pulpit," or "From Prize Fighting to Preaching." There was nothing wrong about these subjects. These men were just telling the world what a great change the new birth had wrought in them. There is no change in all the world so radical as the change of conversion. There are only two classes of people in the world. Those who have been touched and changed, and those who have not.

When Jesus was here He touched people and changed them. The blind received their sight; the crippled were made whole; the demon-possessed ones found a good and happy life. He is still touching people through the new birth. He is making greater changes now than when He was upon the earth. The spiritual changes that He makes in the lives of men today are greater than the physical changes that He made in lives when He was upon the earth.

Two sisters had not seen each other for several years. One of them paid the other a visit. The one whom she visited said, "I don't know what has happened to you, but you are much easier to live with than in the old days." What had happened? She had been born again. There had been some changes made.

We hear someone quote these words, "The things I once loved I now hate; the things I once hated I now love." These words are not found in the Bible, but this truth is seen every day in the lives around us. Here we find a man who once hated the thought of going to church and despised the spiritual things, but God touched his heart one day and now he looks forward to every minute he can spend in the house of the Lord. He has experienced the change of the New Birth.

In John 1:12 you read: "As many as received him, to them gave he the power to become the sons of God." What a change is made when we receive Him and enter His great family. We are lifted out of the miry clay and our feet are set upon a rock. We are freed from the slavery of sin and set upon the throne of blessing.

II. There Is the Change Created by Growth in Grace

"But grow in grace, and in the knowledge of our Lord and Saviour Jesus Christ. To him be glory both now and for ever" (II Peter 3:18).

The pastor's greatest joy is to see lost people saved. His second greatest joy is to see souls growing in grace. What a joy it is to watch young Christians as they grow more like the Master. I have watched them with great interest as they grew from babes in Christ to active and useful servants of the Lord. My daily prayer is, "Lord give us more Christians like these." Some members never grow. They are a great sorrow to their Master and to those who love them. Some members do grow and they are a real joy to the Lord and to those who love them. Which class are you in?

Growth in grace is aided by faithfulness. "I was glad when they said unto me, let us go unto the house of the Lord" (Ps. 122:1). The pupil in the day school grows more, mentally, if he attends school every day than if he attends only once a month. So does the Christian grow more like Christ if he is faithful. I can never understand how one who has been born again and greatly blessed of the Lord can go on for months without darkening the door of the church. If you want to grow in grace and become a more useful Christian and bring more joy to the heart of Jesus, you must be faithful in attendance at His house.

Growth in grace is aided by Bible reading and prayer. Day by day when you read your Bible and pray you must say to yourself: "I must be a better Christian, I must be more like Jesus." Many people say, "I do not know much about the Bible." There is only one reason for this: they never read it. I know nothing about meteorology. Why? Because I have never studied it. Likewise people who never study the Bible know nothing about it. But the Bible is a deep book and if you read it there will be some changes made in your life.

Growth in grace is aided by active service. Physical exercise makes us strong physically, and spiritual exercise will cause us to grow in grace. Be faithful in your Christian duties; read the Bible and pray; serve the Lord actively all the time; then you will grow in grace and in the knowledge of the Lord Jesus Christ.

III. There Is the Change Created by Prayer

"And as he prayed, the fashion of his countenance was altered, and his raiment was white and glistering" (Luke 9:29).

Prayer changed even Jesus, and it will change you inside and out.

Sometime ago I attended a revival service in a great church. In the foyer of the church there was a sign which read, "Prayer Changes Things." Inside the church I heard a man preach and saw people saved, and I went away saying, "Prayer changes people, too."

Do you remember the old song, "Mother's Prayers Have Followed Me"? Many a boy has gone into the world and has forgotten God and entered into a life of sin, but his mother was still praying for him and one day a great change came. He was saved and life was made over for him. The change had been created because of prayer.

Stonewall Jackson in the midst of war was still a great Christian. He said that he had fixed the habit of prayer in his mind so that he never raised a glass of water to his lips without asking a blessing. He never sealed a letter but that he prayed for the one to whom the letter was going. When he was a teacher he said that as the classes were changing he would pray for the cadets who were coming in and those who were going out. James Gilmour, the great missionary, never used a blotter. He wrote his letters and then prayed while he was waiting for the ink to dry.

Habits like these oblige us to change our lives. Prayer brings peace to a troubled heart; prayer makes us clean up our lives. If we pray there will be some changes made.

IV. The Greatest Change Will Come When Jesus Comes Back for Us

"Behold, I show you a mystery; we shall not all sleep, but we shall all be changed, in a moment, in the twinkling of an eye, at the last trump: for the trumpet shall sound, and the dead shall be raised incorruptible, and we shall all be changed" (I Cor. 15:51-52).

A certain preacher said, "I know nothing about the Second Coming of Christ." And yet about one fourth of the Bible is taken up with this great truth. A man who says he knows nothing about it is saying that he knows nothing about the Bible. I do not profess to know all the mysteries of the future, but it is sweet to go to the Bible and study the plain teachings of Christ about His coming again.

When is He coming? We do not know — the angels in heaven do not know. But upon the great calendar of eternity God has circled a certain day. On that day Jesus will be coming back for those who love Him.

"He will come at the last trump." This is a military figure. In the olden days when the first trumpet was blown the soldiers packed up their tents and weapons. When the second trumpet blew they fell in line. They marched away at the blowing of the third or last trumpet. If we study prophecy and what Jesus says is going to happen, and if we look into the world today, we are sure that the first two trumpets must have already sounded and it may not be long until the last trump shall blow. Can you say, "I am ready for His coming?" Can you say with John, "Even so, come Lord Jesus?"

What will happen to us when He comes in the air? Listen to these great words in I Thessalonians 4:16-17: "For the Lord himself shall descend from heaven with a shout, with the voice of the archangel, and with the trump of God: and the dead in Christ shall rise first: then we which are alive and remain shall be caught up together with them in the clouds, to meet the Lord in the air: and so shall we ever be with the Lord." At that hour Jesus will come: the dead in Christ shall rise up to meet Him; and the Christians who are down in the world will be caught up to complete the group. What a blessed time of reunion that will be!

Now the text tells us that we shall be changed. What kind

of change will this be? Why, it will be the change that every true Christian longs to have. It will be a change into the glorious likeness of the Lord Jesus Christ. "Beloved, now are we the sons of God, and it doth not yet appear what we shall be: but we know that, when he shall appear, we shall be like him; for we shall see him as he is."

Will it not be wonderful to be like Jesus? When we look at the life that He lived and then at the one we are living it seems that we are often poles apart. But in that day we shall mount up to be with Him and we shall be changed and made to be just like Him. Oh, what a wonderful Saviour! In Him there is no sin but all is life and light. I have seen some good Christians, but none like Jesus. Thank God in that day, we shall be changed and we shall all be like Him in every way.

Have you ever said about some person, "I don't believe I could live, even in heaven, with that man?" Maybe he feels the same way about you. But if you are a believer in Christ you will be changed when He comes. You will be made like unto Him. All of our bad points will be gone then and we will live in perfect harmony with each other.

How long will it take for this change to come about? Why, it will happen in the twinkling of an eye. We are told that this is the swiftest movement of the human body. When the dead are raised incorruptible and when the living are taken up into the air to meet Jesus, we shall all be changed in the twinkling of an eye. Are you ready for that time? Are you trusting Him? Are you loving Him and serving Him? If so, that will be the greatest moment of your life. If not, may God have mercy on your soul.

Yes, we are living in a world of change, but there is One who never changes. He is the "same yesterday, today and forever."

> Change and decay in all around I see,
> Oh, thou who changest not, abide with me!

He never changes. He never changes in His love, in His Gospel or in His saving power. He is the changeless Christ for a changing world. Is He the Saviour of your heart?

When I was pastor of the Broadway Baptist Church, Knoxville, Tennessee, a certain man ran a grocery store just across the street from the church. Someone said to me one day, "That man is drinking himself to death. He is ruining his business and breaking the hearts of his wife and little girl." I went over to see him and invited him to come to our church. He began coming on Sunday nights. One night when the sermon had been preached and the invitation had been given, he came down the aisle, brushing the tears out of his eyes, and confessed Christ as his Saviour.

Sometime after that my wife and I visited this man's home on Sunday afternoon. He was out in the back yard playing with his little girl. I left the ladies in the house and went out into the back yard. When that man saw me coming, he took his little girl by the hand and started to meet me. I said to him, "How is it with you now?" and he replied, "I am the happiest man in all the world. I didn't know that life could hold so much joy for a human being. Everything is changed since I found Christ as my Saviour." Today he is a deacon and a useful member of that church.

The change always comes when we allow Jesus to come into our hearts. He knocks at the door of your heart today. He can change your life, your future, your destiny — if you surrender to Him. And then some day He will change you into His own glorious likeness and bear you spotless before the Throne. Oh, come to Him today and let the change begin in you even now!

9

Getting off the Beam

And the world passeth away, and the lust thereof: but he that doeth the will of God abideth for ever (I John 2:17).

Aviation is one of the most fascinating sciences in the world. With every passing year new discoveries are being made in the realm of aeronautics. One of the marvels of science is the radio beam, which the pilot uses regularly, but especially when he is likely to get off the course because of bad weather or darkness. Here is a plane going from Los Angeles to New York. A terrible storm comes up, and the pilot cannot see where he is going. Now a radio beam shoots out between these two stations. The pilot finds this beam and sticks to the course and lands safely at his destination. If he goes off to one side, the beam flashes a warning and he brings his ship back into the right place. If he goes too far off he gets into danger and this deviation may result in the wrecking of his plane.

Now for the Christian this "beam" is the will of God, or God's plan for his life. The text tells us that "whosoever doeth the will of God abideth forever." If you stay on the "beam" of His will, you will be happy and useful and arrive safely at your destination. If you get "off the beam," you lose your influence, your power, your usefulness and your spiritual happiness.

I. You Get off the Beam When You
Neglect Simple Christian Duties

There are some fundamental duties such as church attendance, tithing, living a consecrated life and serving God day by day. When you neglect these simple duties you are "getting off the beam."

Here are two men who join the same church. One man goes to church every Sunday, supports God's work with his means and engages in good service for Him. The other man seldom enters the church. The records show that he gives nothing in a whole year's time. He is busy in other things and has no time for the Lord's service. Which one lives closer to God and His will? Which one has a greater influence for good? Which one is the happier and the more useful Christian? You know the answer. God has simply made us so that it takes these things to develop our Christian characters.

A missionary returned from New Guinea and someone asked him, "What did you find when you arrived there?" He replied, "I found a hopeless situation. The people were worse than beasts. Often if a baby began to cry, the mother would become angry and throw it in the ditch and leave it to die. If a man saw his father break his leg he would leave him on the side of the road to die . . . People simply had no compassion and no moral sense." "Well, did you preach to them?" he was asked. "No," the missionary replied, "I did not preach, I just lived. When I saw a baby crying I picked it up and comforted it. When I saw a man with a broken leg I mended it. I took care of them in the best way possible, and when they asked me why I did it, I had a chance to preach the Gospel to them." "Did you succeed?" the man asked. "Yes, when I left New Guinea, I left a thriving church in that community."

You can see, then, that a **good** Christian life is effective.

If you want to be the best Christian, if you want to have the most influence, you do not have to preach. Just look after your Christian duties. Stay on the job and be faithful to Him. You have a duty to your church to give and to live just as much as the preacher. The soldier owes a duty to his country, the engineer must be faithful to his engine and the pilot gives his best to his plane. So must the Christian give his best to the simple Christian duties of life. You get "off the beam" when you are not faithful to them.

II. You Get Off the Beam When You Neglect Prayer and Bible Reading

God has given us these means to help us, to strengthen us and to keep us on the right track. I can tell when a man is reading his Bible and praying, for I can see a change in his life. He grows in grace; he is more interested in his church; he is not criticizing and gossiping; he is working for the interests of the kingdom.

In one pastorate we had a sign which we placed in front of our church. The sign said, "This Church is Open — Come in — Rest and Pray." Many people were encouraged to stop a minute and lift up their hearts to God for spiritual strength. We know that a Christian gets "off the beam" when he neglects his prayer life.

In 1940 I attended the World's Fair in New York City. Over at one of the buildings there was a time capsule which was being filling with the various things of our 1940 life. The capsule was to be buried for five thousand years and then taken up so that the life of that distant day could be compared with the life of 1940. I was glad to notice that a Holy Bible had been placed in the center of the articles that were to be placed in the capsule. Here are the various things in your life — in the center of these things there should be the Bible and prayer. These are two great anchors of the soul. When you get away from them you get "off the beam."

III. You Get Off the Beam When You Get Angry

All of us are guilty right here. Something comes up that goes against us and we boil over like a pot of water on a hot fire. We are "off the beam" then. We are not showing the Christian spirit which we ought to have.

"But," you say, "this is the way it is with me. I get angry, but it is soon over." That may be true, but think of how much damage you do yourself and others in the few minutes that you are angry. Billy Sunday said, "It is like the discharge of a shotgun. It takes only a minute, but it destroys everything near it." So it is with our evil tempers. There is more of Satan in us than there is of Christ when we lose our tempers.

I used to work at a storage battery company. In the back of the building we had shelves where the automobile batteries were placed to be charged. These batteries were filled with acid, and the acid often spilled out and ate away the wooden shelves. In like manner, anger eats away the sweetness of our religion, the peace of our hearts and the power of our influence. You get "off the beam" when you get angry.

IV. You Get Off the Beam When You Have an Unforgiving Spirit

The unforgiving spirit is certainly the unchristian spirit. The Bible tells us not to let the sun go down on our wrath. We are told to forgive seventy times seven times. We are never told to get even nor to hold malice in our hearts. Jesus on the Cross is a supreme example of the real Christian spirit. His enemies were putting Him to death, but still He could say, "Father, forgive them for they know not what they do." We have never been as badly mistreated as He was and yet we often have an unforgiving spirit. Even though a man should knock you down and spit in your face, if you are a Christian you must still forgive him.

A certain man was sick and was told that he was dying. He called in his enemy and offered him his forgiveness. In a few minutes they were rejoicing in a period of sweet fellowship. But the sick man said, "Now, just remember if I do get well, the old grudge still holds." Why not forgive and forget and really mean it?

When is a human soul at its strongest? Is it when we worship in our regular pew? Is it when we kneel and pray? Is it when we read the Bible? No. I think that the human soul is at its best when it is forgiving an injury and putting its revenge aside. This forgiveness is like the scent of sweet flowers when they are trampled upon.

It is said that during the Boxer uprising in China, Christians prayed for those who were killing them. One of the killers came to see a missionary and said to him, "Religion like that really has something in it. Please tell me about it." Oh, when we have a forgiving spirit people are going to see it; they are going to know that we have a real religion! If you have an unforgiving spirit in your heart you are "off the beam." Get it out today and get back "on the beam" of God's way for your life.

V. You Get Off the Beam When You Quit Serving God

I have heard people say, "The Church doesn't need me." The Church needs every single member to help carry on its work. There are many spokes in the wheel, but if any spoke is broken the wheel is that much weakened. Here we see one hundred men in the line of battle, but if one falls out the company is that much weakened. Whoever you are, if you are not in your place, you are weakening the Church just that much. Some people serve God simply by being faithful. Do not think you are of little importance if you are not holding a high job in the Church. Some little people mean more to the kingdom simply by being faithful than many others do who are failing God in their loyalty.

Many Christians served God well in other days; they were "on the beam" then; but now they are "off the beam" and their lives are not counting for Him. I can think of some in my own church. They used to come to church every Sunday; they put in their tithes every week; they served well in various places; but now they never come, and God seems to be left out of all their plans. Surely the real Christian does not feel right when he is not serving God. You are "off the beam" if you are not busy for Him every day.

VI. You Get Off the Beam When You Seek Happiness Elsewhere Except in Jesus and in His Service

This old world is filled with unhappy people. They have no stabilizing influence in their lives today. They have no hope in their lives for tomorrow. They are hungry-hearted people in every way. They are looking for happiness, but they are looking for it in the wrong places. They seek it in the world, in pleasures, in the pursuit of material things. They are "off the beam." Happiness is found only in Christ and in His service. A dying man was laughing and smiling, and his doctor said to him, "Man, don't you realize you are dying?" "Yes," said the man, "but that is all right. Years ago I met a man who taught me how to smile and I can smile even in death because of Him — His name is Jesus."

Poor sinners, poor carnal Christians who are looking for happiness and cannot find it! You are looking for it out in the world, when it is found only in Jesus Christ. Come and serve Him, and in Him and in His service you will find happiness that the world cannot give you and the world cannot take away. You do not look for warmth at the North Pole, nor for icebergs in Florida. Yet you are looking for your happiness in the wrong places. You are "off the beam." Look for happiness in the service of Christ and you will surely find it.

VII. You Get Off the Beam When You Fail to Trust God Completely

He wants us to trust Him completely, and most of us are guilty right here. Some trouble comes up and we begin to worry and not trust.

There are two things which ought to make us trust God. First, we ought to trust Him because He promises to care for us. A husband promises to care for his wife and she trusts him to do that. A father promises to feed and clothe his children and they trust him for it. God's Book is full of promises to care for us and He always keeps His promises. A man may fail in his promises, but God never does — you can trust Him.

Second, past experiences ought to make us trust God. We look back over life and remember how He brought us out of our trouble so many times. He has done it before and we know that He will do it again. David said, "I cried unto God . . . and he gave ear unto me" (Ps. 77:1). We can say that, too, for we have had that experience. We know that we can trust Him to care for us in the future as He has done in the past. When you fail to trust Him you are getting "off the beam." It is His will for you to look up into His face and trust Him implicitly.

VIII. You Get Off the Beam Every Time You Sin

God's line is a straight line. When you get off that line you are sinning and you are "off the beam." Many a plane crash has been charged to the fact that the pilot was off the beam. If you get "off the beam" and get into sin it may mean the wrecking of your whole life.

A man was laid up in the hospital with a broken leg. When asked how it happened, he said, "I slipped on a little spot of ice. I went out of my way a whole block to avoid an icy street, but right in front of my home I slipped on a tiny spot and it threw me." So it is that a man often walks along carefully, and then a little sin creeps into his life. He slips and his whole future is wrecked. Yes, we get "off the beam" when we sin.

Too many people blame their sin on their environment or their companions. A preacher tells of going into a mining district where everything was dirty and dingy. He saw coal dust on every house, every tree and every blade of grass. But near the mine he found a beautiful white flower, clean and pure. He said to a friend, "The owner of that flower must take good care of it to keep it free from dirt and dust." "No," said the man, "that isn't the secret." He then took a handful of coal dust and threw it right on the flower. The dust fell to the ground and the flower was as clean and as pure as ever. "You see," said the man, "the flower has an enamel which prevents the dirt from clinging to it, and that is the reason it is clean."

If Jesus is in your heart you have the greatest prevention in the world against sin and you can go anywhere and with anyone and yet you do not have to sin. The Psalmist said, "Thy word have I hid in mine heart, that I might not sin against thee" (Ps. 119:11). Yes, if we keep Him and His word, we can overcome all sin.

But every time you sin in deed or word or thought you can say, "I am off the beam — I am not in the will of God."

My friend, are you "off the beam" in any way? Well, you can get back on. When a plane gets off the beam the pilot finds it out and gets back on the beam as soon as possible. Come and confess your sin and find your place in God's service and stay faithfully in that place until He calls you home.

A boy and his mother one day passed a candy store. At his request the mother gave the boy a penny. He went into the store and walked up and down before all the show cases that were filled with good candy. The mother opened the door and said, "Hurry, son." And the boy replied, "but, mother, I have but one penny to spend and I want to spend it in the right way." Oh, my friends, we have just one life to spend. Let us be careful to spend it in the right way. Let us find God's place for our lives and let us live always for Him. We are His, created in His image and redeemed by the blood of His Son. God help us to get "on the beam" and to do what He put us here to do!

10

Back to Bethel

And God said unto Jacob, Arise, go up to Bethel, and dwell
there: and make there an altar unto God, that appeared unto
thee when thou fleddest from the face of Esau thy brother
(Gen. 35:1).

Jacob is one of the strangest characters in the Bible. Someone has said that he is the worst and the best man in the Old
Testament. When we see him cheating his brother, Esau,
out of his birthright, he is at his worst; when we hear him
making his vows unto God after his vision of the ladder and
the angels, he is at his best. When he puts on an animal skin
and deceives his father, Isaac, he is at his worst; when he
wrestles with the angel and pleads for a blessing, he is at
his best.

After his sin against Esau, Jacob's mother advised him to
flee. He left his home in a hurry, and he spent his first night
under the stars with a stone for a pillow. It was there that
God appeared to him in a vivid way. The next morning he
made his vow, saying, "This is my God and I will follow
Him all the days of my life, and of all that which He gives to
me I will give the tenth unto Him." He went on his way;
he became rich; he forgot God and the vows he made at Bethel.
The years go by and now he is coming home. He has another
experience with God: he wrestles with the angel and prevails.
He meets Esau and Esau forgives and forgets. But Jacob is not

yet filled with peace, for his sin is still on his heart. Then it is that God calls him: "Go back to Bethel. Go back where you made your vow, back where you first felt My presence. Go back and renew your vows and start life over again."

Jacob was glad to go. He had sinned deeply and felt the need of God's mercy. He had cheated others and had been cheated. Life held no peace of heart for him for he had sinned too greatly. He felt the need of God. He heard God's call and went back to Bethel and rededicated his life in that holy place.

Today many of us are far away from God. Back in the years gone by we remember our Bethel. We had an experience with God. He touched us and saved us, but the years have come and gone and they have taken away some of our spiritual freshness. We have neglected our duty, and we have back-slidden. We have lost the joy of our salvation, and so today we cry out:

> Where is the blessedness I knew,
> When first I met my Lord?

No matter how far you have gone away from Him, God still loves you and still calls you. You are so busy with the world that you cannot hear Him, but He is still calling and you should answer in the words of the song:

> Back to Bethel I must go,
> Back where the rivers of sweet waters flow.
> Back to the true life my soul longs to know,
> Bethel is calling, and I must go.

Back to Bethel — what does it mean to us today?

I. BACK TO BETHEL MEANS BACK TO A REMEMBRANCE OF OUR FIRST LOVE

Jacob's first love was for God, but he had forgotten Him in the mad rush. Surely we love Him best of all, too, but we often are indifferent to Him. In the Revelation Jesus rebuked a certain church, saying to it, "You have left your first love." That is true of many of us. Once we found our highest joy in serving Jesus, but some of us have been drifting with the tide. Other loves have entered and God has been left outside of our hearts in the cold.

A Christian man was saying good-by to his son. He put his hand upon his shoulder and said to him, "Wherever you go, always remember whose son you are." Wherever we go we should remember that we belong to God, that He is our first love. When temptations come our way, let us say, "I cannot do this thing, for I belong to God."

Here is a girl who has many boy friends. But one day the right one comes along. She loves him with all her heart and surrenders to him. He must go away for a while, but he knows that her heart is his. While he is away others come in and they want to claim a part of her love, but she says, "No, it's all for him." She is true to her love every second of her life. We go along in life and this old sinful world is our friend, but then Jesus comes into our hearts and we surrender to Him. Satan comes along and says, "Give me a part of your life," and always we should say to him, "No, Jesus has the first place in my heart and life." What a pity that it has not been that way. Many of us have forsaken our first love and today we love some of the things of Satan more than we do the things of God. But God is calling us back to Bethel and back to our first love.

What did Jacob say to his family when he started toward Bethel? Here it is: "Put away the strange gods that are among you" (Gen. 35:2). They gave up their strange gods, and Jacob buried them under an oak. We need to dig a grave for our false gods. We need to tear them out of our lives and bury them forever.

Back to your first love means back to the right life and the right spirit. It means back to a life where God is put above all else in all things. Lord Melbourne went to church in London one day. When the sermon was over he rushed out of the church saying, "That preacher is a fool. He seems to think that religion has something to do with a practical personal life." My friends, it does. We ought to get back to our first love and carry God with us in every walk of life.

A boy in Minnesota died of diptheria. His family cleaned out the house and fumigated every room, except a small closet which was never used. They then moved back into the house. Some days later a shawl was taken from the closet and wrapped around one of the children when they went out to see friends. There was a diptheria germ in that shawl. The disease broke out again and three lives were lost. My friends, sin is more deadly than a diptheria germ. We cannot afford simply to clean up a part of our lives and leave the spots that will destroy our spiritual strength. We need to clean it all up and come back to God.

II. Back to Bethel Means Back to the Better Life We Once Knew

A child climbed up into his father's lap and asked, "Daddy, is God dead?" The father answered, "Why do you ask that, my child?" The little boy said, "Well, I don't hear you talking to Him any more." The father dropped his head upon his bosom in shame. Do you recall how you used to pray? Have you quit praying. God is not dead but He might as well be for many people, for they never pray.

A young man was led to the electric chair and with his last words he said, "If I had had the right kind of father and mother, this would never have happened." A gambler in the penitentiary said, "My father was to blame. When I was a child he taught me to drink and curse." Oh, if our parents are people of prayer, these things will not happen! But you know how it is. Parents go on and on and forget God and never pray, and then in their hours of trouble they cry out unto Him.

> O, what peace we often forfeit,
> O, what needless pain we bear,
> All because we do not carry
> Everything to God in prayer.

An eccentric country preacher, going along a country road, stopped at a beautiful home. He wondered if the people there were Christians. He knocked on the door and when the woman came to the door he asked, "Madam, does Jesus live here?" She was absolutely astounded and could not reply. He repeated the question and still she could say nothing. The old preacher went on down the road. That night the woman told her husband about this amazing experience. "Didn't you tell him we belonged to the church?" he asked. "No," she replied, "he didn't ask about that." "Didn't you tell him that we gave our money to the church?" "No," she said, "he didn't want to know about these things. He wanted to know if Jesus lived here, and that is different."

It is different. I do not ask about your membership and your gifts, but I do ask you this question: Does Jesus live in your heart and home? Go back to Bethel and throw yourself at His feet and pour your heart out and pray to Him.

III. Back to Bethel Means Back to the Bible

Henry Van Dyke said, "A man who has been through one hundred high schools and universities and who does not know the Bible is not an educated man and never can be." Daniel Webster said, "The Bible is the secret of the blessing which rests upon our country. If we neglect it our doom will be sudden and complete."

A minister taught an old man to read. Later on he met the old man's wife and asked her, "How is your husband getting along with his reading?" "Fine," she replied. "I guess he can read the Bible well by now, can't he?" asked the minister. "Oh, he is out of the Bible and into the newspaper now," said the woman. I am afraid that is true of too many of us today. We have graduated from the Bible into every other kind of reading matter in the world, and God's Word is neglected and our souls are drying up.

A ship was wrecked in the South Seas. The sailors climbed into the small boats and pushed off. Suddenly two of them jumped in the water and swam back to the sinking ship. They had forgotten the compass. It was the only guide through the unknown waters, and it was worth risking their lives to get it. The Bible is our compass and our guide, and we cannot afford to neglect it. Yet too many Christians have laid it aside and the dust settles on it and it is never read.

What would you do without the Bible? You may not read it, but today you are enjoying the many blessings that it has brought to the world. Science and philosophy and worldly wisdom cannot answer our deepest questions. Here is a widow who has lost her only son. She wants to know if she will ever see him again. Let science answer her. "Science," we say, "we have put away the Bible. We want a scientific answer. Will this woman ever see her son again?" But there is no answer. Science and philosophy have nothing to say. Baffled by it all we fall back on the Bible and we hear that great Book saying, "I am the resurrection, and the life: he that believeth in me, though he were dead, yet shall he live," (John 11:25) "So shall we ever be with the Lord" (I Thess. 4:17) "I go to prepare a place for you" (John 14:2). "This corruptible must put on incorruption" (I Cor. 15:53). The Bible is the only book that can answer life's great questions for us. We cannot put it away. Back to Bethel means back to the Bible.

IV. BACK TO BETHEL MEANS BACK TO ACTIVE SERVICE
FOR THE LORD

Jacob went back to Bethel and from that day on he lived a life of faithful service.

Sometime ago I was riding along a road in North Carolina. By the side of the road I saw a piece of road machinery that had been left there many, many months before. It had been used to build this mountain road, but now it was set aside and was absolutely useless and in the way. Many Christians are like that. Once they were active — they led in great spiritual movements, they taught large Bible classes, they backed up the pastor in a great program — but now they have quit their work and they are doing nothing for the Lord or man. I heard sometime ago of a man who once had a Sunday school class running into the thousands. But the years have come and gone and now he takes no active part in the work of the kingdom. We talk about the "has-beens" in baseball. They are the men who once played a great game, but who are not equal to it today. We have too many "has-beens" in our churches. Oh, for men who actually serve God all of the days of their lives!

Do your remember the first service that you gave to Christ? It brought you unspeakable joy, but you have drifted out of this service. You have tried everything else and there has been no happiness in it. Bethel calls you back today to a happy and active service.

Sometimes it takes a great sorrow to bring us back to Bethel. We go merrily on our way forgetting God until we are shrouded with the pall of death or suffering. Then we cry out, "Oh God!" But joy comes to us when we go back to Bethel. It came to Jacob and it will come to us.

Sometime ago one of my members, who was the express agent in our city, told me that at dawn of a certain morning he would release some carrier pigeons that had been shipped from a loft thousands of miles away. I went with him to the station. The coop of pigeons was taken from the railroad car in which they had been traveling, the agent released the door of the coop and the pigeons flew out and straight into the air. They circled around several times, then headed straight to their home loft. The next day a telegram came saying they had arrived safely. The pigeons did not belong in a lowly coop.

Neither do we as Christians belong on the low plains of a worldly life. Bethel is our home and Jesus is our first love. Let us today take our bearings and head straight toward the heavenly home; let us remember our first love; let us go back to a good prayer life. Let us make the Bible again our daily companion and let us give our days in active service to the Lord.

In a certain cathedral in Denmark is a large marble statue of Christ. A cynical man came into the cathedral one day and stood in the back of the building. He said to the scrub woman, "I see nothing great about that statue." The scrub woman said, "You must go a little closer." He walked a little way down the aisle and the woman said again, "You must go a little closer." Three times this happened until at last he was standing at the base of the statue and looking up into the face of Jesus. He looked for a long time and then read the inscription on the base of the statue, "Come unto me, all ye that labour and are heavy laden, and I will give you rest." The man fell down upon his knees crying out, "My Lord and my God!"

Are you far away from Christ today? God is calling you to come closer, to come to Bethel, to come and learn anew of the beauty and love and greatness of Jesus. Then go out to serve Him until He calls you home.

11

The "I Will's" of Jesus

Nevertheless I tell you the truth; it is expedient for you
that I go away: for if I go not away, the Comforter will not
come unto you; but if I depart, I will send him unto you
(John 16:7).

Sometime ago one business man said this about another
one: "His word is as good as his bond." It is fine when men
can say this of you. Another business man had as his motto
the words, "I always do what I say I will do." We cannot say
this of many men for they often disappoint us. They make
their promises and never keep them. They give their word and
never make it good. But there is One upon whose Word you
can always depend — Jesus. When Jesus says "I will" we
may know that it will surely be done. He has promised certain
things to us in the Bible. He has done some of them already,
he is doing others now, and He will do still others in the
future. Let us think today about the "I wills" of Jesus.

I. THE "I WILL" OF SALVATION

"Him that cometh to me I will in no wise cast out"
(John 6:37).

This is the promise of reception for sinners. Jesus is simply
saying that no matter who you are or what your sins are
like, nor how far you have gone from God, if you will simply

come to Jesus, He will not cast you out. If you try to join certain clubs you must have a certain amount of money. If you wish to join a certain lodge they may "black-ball" you. If you would like to become a member of certain civic organizations they have no room for you. But Jesus makes no such restrictions. The amount of money will not matter; He will never "black-ball" you; He will always have room for you. His only requirement is this: "Him that cometh to me." This means that you are to leave your sin in true repentance and to place all your faith in Jesus as Saviour.

> Come ye sinners, poor and needy,
> Weak and wounded, sick and sore;
> Jesus ready stands to save you,
> Full of pity, love, and power.

A young soldier who had been living a sinful, careless life became a Christian. Everyone noted the great change in his life and asked him how it came about. He replied, "Jesus Christ said to me, 'Right about face,' and I obeyed Him in my heart." That is conversion — turning *from* the world and its sin *to* Christ the Saviour. If you are not a child of God today, whatever your sin may be, this is His "I will" for you — He simply says, "Come to me, leave all your sin — take me as your Saviour and I will not cast thee out."

II. The "I Will" of the Church's Foundation

"Upon this rock I will build my church" (Matt. 16:18).

Jesus was talking to His disciples one day and His climax question was this: "Whom do ye say that I am?" One of them replied, "Thou art the Christ, the son of the living God." Then Jesus said, "Upon this rock — the rock of my divine Sonship — I will build my Church, and the gates of hell will not prevail against it."

Christ has been building that Church ever since. Every time a man comes and says, "I believe in Christ; I am trusting

in Him," Christ takes that man and uses him as another
brick in the great building. You may say, "He is building
out of poor material when He uses poor human lives." Yes,
that is true, but remember that He is the foundation and
for that reason the Church can never fail. It is a divine thing
and will stand forever.

What did Christ mean by the gates of hell? He was
speaking of all the powers of evil in this world. These powers
have been blasting at the Church through the centuries but
it stands just as staunch as ever. Look at all the evil
institutions in the world today. Their proprietors would not
admit it, but they are working against all that the Church
stands for. They come and go but the Church lives on.

The Church stands today because it offers what no other
institution can offer. The Church offers forgiveness of sin to
the sinful soul; it offers peace of heart to the troubled; it
offers strength to the weak for every mile of the way; it
offers a blessed hope for the life to come. It can offer all
of these things because it is Christ's Church — the one agency
in the world through which He has chosen to do His work.

There are other good agencies in the world, but the Church
is peculiarly Christ's own. My fear is that many church
members are giving too much time to man-made institutions
and not enough time and effort to the only institution which
Christ founded and through which He promises to do His
work — the Church.

I love to think of how the Church has stood for two
thousand years. It met first behind locked doors for fear
of its persecutors. It met later in the catacombs of Rome.
But the Church had the Spirit of Christ in it and it could
not be conquered nor destroyed. Down through the ages,
somewhere in the world, groups of people who loved the Lord
have made and kept the Church going — and it will go on

forever, either as the Church militant on earth or the Church triumphant in heaven.

Jesus said, "I will build my Church." Are you helping Him in this great task? Are you a part of the Church through faith in Christ? Are you bearing your part of the load? Are you building up or tearing down? Are you seeking to bring others into the shelter of its fold? Thank God for His Church. There is no institution in the world so powerful, so purposeful, so permanent.

III. The "I Will" of the Holy Spirit

"I will send him unto you" (John 16:7).

Jesus here is leaving His disciples. He has told them that He is going to die, and He has looked into their sorrow-laden faces. With great compassion He says to them, "I will not leave you alone; I will send my Spirit unto you. Just wait and pray and one day He will come." They prayed for ten days and on Pentecost the Spirit came to them. He is here today in the hearts of all those who believe in Christ. I like the simple definition: "the Holy Spirit is God living in the hearts of believers."

What is the Spirit's work on earth? First of all, He convicts of sin. A man with sin in his heart goes on and on hardly realizing that he is a sinner. Then one day the Holy Spirit turns His light into the black heart and the man sees it as a den of evil and wrong. He wants to do something about it, and the Holy Spirit leads him to the foot of the Cross and points him to Christ.

The Holy Spirit guides the Christian. There are many crossroads in life and we know not which road to take. But we need not go by chance, the Christian prays for guidance and the Holy Spirit points out the best way for him.

The Holy Spirit comforts the bereaved. Jesus called Him

the Comforter. When sorrow comes we are not like orphans, for we have a Holy Spirit who is like a tender mother, who puts His arms around us and speaks words of comfort unto our hearts.

The Holy Spirit helps us to understand the Bible. In my home I have a cozy chair in the corner of the living room. I sometimes sit there and read in the evening. I try to read by the light that comes in from a western window, but I find that light to be too dim; so I reach over and turn on an electric lamp that has been placed on the table by the side of my easy chair. Immediately I can see clearly every letter and every word. In like manner we try to read the Bible by our own dim intelligence, and its pages have little meaning for us; but when we turn on the light of God's Holy Spirit, those deep truths are brightly illuminated and we understand as we can never do otherwise.

The Holy Spirit inspires and enpowers us for service. He brings fruit into our lives. When we serve in our own strength we can do nothing, but when we have Him to empower us our service really counts.

Jesus said, "I will send my Spirit." What if He had not come? You and I would be groping in spiritual darkness without God and without hope in the world. Thank God, Jesus did send His Holy Spirit.

IV. THE "I WILL" OF CONSTANT COMPANIONSHIP

"Lo, I am (will be) with you alway, even unto the end of the world" (Matt. 28:20).

Jesus had risen from the dead. Forty days He had been upon the earth and now He is going back to the Father's home. He gives to His disciples explicit directions as to how His work is to be done and then He says, "I will be with you unto the end of the way." There is great encouragement here for every Christian worker. As you stand to preach or teach or sing you know that you are not alone, but that you have the presence and power of the living Christ.

I believe that this text goes further than this. Jesus is interested in every phase of our lives and He promises to be with us everywhere. As you go to your place of business He goes there with you. He is particularly interested in the things of the home. He goes with the young people to school, and out into every walk of life with each of us.

After many years in Africa, David Livingston returned to Oxford where he received an honorary degree. He stood before the students in the chapel and told of his life in the Dark Continent. He stood there with his limp arm hanging by his side, an arm that had been made helpless by the savage attack of a lion. He told of the long days and the lonely nights, the months when he never saw a white man's face. Then he said, "I will tell you what sustained me — it was the promise of Jesus where He said, 'I will be with you!' I could not have gone on if I had not felt that Christ Himself was walking by my side."

James Hilton has written a book, We Are Not Alone. Oh, beloved, remember this: we are never alone! Always, everywhere, from the time we give our hearts to Him until the time when we rest with Him in glory, we have a wonderful companion and His name is Jesus!

V. The "I Will" of His Magnetic Power

"And I, if I be lifted up from the earth, will draw all men unto me" (John 12:32).

He was lifted up, and He has been drawing men ever since. He draws the black and white, the rich and the poor, the high and the low — He draws all men. Are we not glad that He drew us? We were in sin, going down to our doom, but one day we felt His drawing power; we yielded to Him; we came and knelt at His pierced feet and great joy and peace filled our souls.

> O happy day that fixed my choice
> On Thee, my Saviour and my God.

He draws in various ways. You go to church and hear a gospel sermon. Your heart is deeply moved and you may go away and forget, but Christ is drawing. You may be seriously sick and in your darkest moments you promise God that if He will give you back your health you will serve Him. You get well and forget the promise — yet Christ was drawing. You go to a funeral and bear about the hope which the Christian has and you say, "I have been too busy about other things; the main thing is to be a Christian. I am not ready, but someday my time will come. I must remember and get ready." You go back to your office, and business cares crowd in upon you and you put the whole thing out of your mind. You go back to the old rut and God is forgotten — yet He was drawing.

VI. The "I Will" of the Blessed Hope

"I will come again" (John 14:3).

Jesus went home to heaven and to the Father's house. Those who loved Him remained here in a troubled world. Is there no hope for us then? Yes, He is coming back after us some day. This is our blessed hope. He is coming to take us home with Him where we shall be forever more. Once I rather shrank from the thought of His coming. I thought of my home and my work and my loved ones, and I did not want to leave them. But His coming will not break up these things; it will only serve to make them perfect and complete. He will take us to a better home and give us better work and give our loved ones to us in a land where we will never part again.

Moses wept because he was not going to be allowed the

privilege of entering the Promised Land, but I am sure God must have said, "Moses, I have something better for you than this. I have a Promised Land that far surpasses this one." There are many good things in God's world. Those friends are very precious, but is heaven not better than this world, and is Christ's company not better than that of anyone else?

In the story of the talents you remember that Jesus said, "Well done, thou good and faithful servant: thou hast been faithful over a few things, I will make thee ruler over many things" (Matt. 25:21). Yes, He promises that if we suffer with Him here, we will rule with Him there. Do you ever feel that the burden is too heavy to bear? Would you like to leave it all behind and go and find peace somewhere? You will never feel that way after He comes, for then every troublesome thing shall be done away with. We will have perfect bodies, perfect minds, perfect hearts, perfect friends, and perfect fellowship with a perfect Saviour.

The Motion Picture Academy gives awards each year to the best actors and actresses. The 1940 decisions were kept secret until the evening of the big banquet. All Hollywood attended this banquet. Millions of dollars worth of jewels were flashing upon the clothing and persons of those who were gathered. The opening address was given over the radio by President Roosevelt. The suspense was so great that many of the glamorous stars in the audience broke down and wept. And what were the awards given? They were simply some gold-plated statues called "Oscars." I am thinking of another event greater than anything in this old world. It is the day of His coming, for He said, "Behold, I come quickly; and my reward is with me, to give to every man according as his work shall be" (Rev. 22:12). Oh, what a day that will be! Lord, hasten His coming!

Beyond the smiling and the weeping,
Beyond the waking and the sleeping,
Beyond the sowing and the reaping,
    I shall be soon.
Love, rest and home, sweet home;
Lord, tarry not, but come.

Beyond the blooming and the fading,
Beyond the shining and the shading,
Beyond the hoping and the dreading,
    I shall be soon.
Love, rest and home, sweet home;
Lord, tarry not, but come.

Beyond the parting and the meeting,
Beyond the farewell and the greeting,
Beyond the pulse's fever beating,
    I shall be soon.
Love, rest and home, sweet home;
Lord, tarry not, but come.   —*Horatius Bonar*

A traveling man in Norway went to see a church in a certain town. Looking up toward the tower he saw there the carved figure of a lamb. He inquired about it and they told him this story. When they were constructing the church, one day a workman high up on a scaffold, lost his hold and began to fall. His fellow workers knew that he would be killed, but he was hurt only slightly. How did this happen? Well, just as he fell a flock of sheep was passing by. He fell among them as they crowded together and his body landed right on top of a lamb. The lamb was crushed to death, but the man was saved. In commemoration of his escape he carved the figure of the lamb on the top of the church.

Oh, brother, Christ is the Lamb slain from the foundation of the world. He was crucified for your sins and mine! He died to save us. As you think of His sacrifice, does not gratitude swell up in your heart? Do you not love Jesus, too?

12

If I Were Satan

Be sober, be vigilant; because your adversary the devil, as a roaring lion, walketh about, seeking whom he may devour (I Peter 5:8).

Back yonder in the eternal ages, before this world began, God lived in heaven with all His angels around Him. But it seems that the one angel highest above all was Satan. His high position made him proud and rebellious against God Himself. Now a thing like that cannot be tolerated in heaven. Pride cannot stand before God, so Satan lost his high position and was cast out of heaven. Satan has never recovered from this downfall, for ever since he has been trying to defeat the purpose and work of God.

What is God's great purpose? It is to save people, and for this purpose He gave His Only-begotten Son to die upon Calvary's Cross. Now the great work of the Devil is in trying to keep people from being saved. If I were Satan and wanted to prevent the salvation of people, what would I do? I would do just what he is doing. He is not a fool; he is a creature of great cunning and intelligence. He knows how to work on people. He has been busy for centuries and will be busy until the end.

119

I. If I Were Satan I Would Deceive People as to Myself

He does just that. In Ephesians 6:11 we read of "the wiles of the devil." He is full of all kinds of tricks. But his greatest trick is this: to make people think that he does not exist. There are some who say that there is no Devil, but if they would try to live just one day for God they would know that the Devil does exist. Modern cartoonists poke fun at a belief in Satan. They paint him as a sinister being arrayed in a red suit, having a long tail and carrying a fork in his hand. But the Devil does not come that way. He comes robed in beauty and light.

The Bible describes Satan as a roaring lion. We have a right to be afraid of him. He is also described as a serpent, a deceiver, the evil one, the dragon. If we saw anyone of these coming toward us we would flee for our lives. Although the Devil comes clad in beauty he is still the same old Devil underneath. His motive is evil only, and we should not let him fool us regarding himself.

When Little Red Riding Hood went into her grandmother's cabin she saw someone in bed dressed in her grandmother's nightgown and cap, but underneath the simple clothing was a big, bad wolf. The Devil clothes himself in many garbs, but he is a ravenous wolf just the same. Yes, if I were Satan I would deceive people about my existence. I would make them believe that I did not exist and while they were denying my existence I would get in my work and lure them downward.

II. If I Were Satan I Would Make Sin Attractive

He does just exactly that. In the Garden of Eden, Eve was surrounded by matchless beauty, but Satan came to turn her from God and he made sin appear so attractive that she yielded. Today he is doing the same thing. He makes sin beautiful to the eye and greatly to be desired and while man yields to temptation he laughs with glee.

Sometime ago I saw a series of pictures. These pictures depicted a young man and young woman tripping along together. There was a chain of roses about them, but as they journeyed on the chain of roses became a chain of steel and at last the Devil is seen dragging them over the cliff to their doom. That is the way he does at first: he makes everything look good and then he leads on until the way of the sinner ends in hell. The Devil gives his best at the first and leads to the worst at the last. God gives His worst at first and we have the best at last.

In II Corinthians 4:4 we are told that "the god of this world hath blinded the minds of them which believe not." As a boy I often set a trap for mice. We used a little round trap. There were several openings in the trap and it was baited with the choicest cheese. I can imagine Jim Mouse as he approaches the trap. "There is no harm here," he says. "The cat is out and the family is asleep. Here is where I get a fine morsel of cheese." He thrusts his head into the trap and as he begins to nibble the cheese the trap springs and breaks his neck. After a while his cousin John Mouse comes along. "Poor Jim," he says, "the trap caught him. But it will never get me." And he thrusts in his head and soon loses his life, too. For centuries Satan has been setting his trap. He fills it with the choicest bait and catches men of every sort. But still there are some who say "Yes, the others got caught, but he will never get me," and they go on in sin and soon they are in his trap.

Look at the places of sin today. They are the most attractive places in town. They reach out their luring hands and pull in their victims. This is the work of Satan.

Now there is a lesson here for the Church. We ought to

make our buildings as attractive and comfortable as possible. Then we can lure men in and tell them of our Blessed Saviour. Yes, if I were Satan I would make sin most attractive.

III. If I Were Satan I Would Hinder God's Word

God's Word is a powerful thing. It sinks into the hearts of men and brings those men to Christ. No wonder the Devil wants to keep the Word out.

A certain man had a bottle inside of which was a pertinent Scripture text. "Why do you keep this?" someone asked, and he replied "I am a deep-sea diver. I found this bottle and this text at the bottom of the ocean. I had long forgotten God, but when I found the bottle, I said, 'If He loves me enough to follow me to the bottom of the ocean, I will yield myself to Him.' " Yes, there is power in the Scriptures to win lost souls.

There was a time when the Bible was chained to the pulpits of England. It could not get out to the people. Satan liked that. He hates for the Word to go out into the human heart. We are told that just after World War I many thousands of people in Russia turned to Christ. What brought about this great revival? It was simple this: the Bible had been made a free and open book in that country.

In His parable of the sower, Jesus tells that some seed fell by the wayside and the birds came along and plucked it up. Often we sow the seed of the Word in the Church here and the Devil plucks it out of the hearts of the people before they can reach home. You hear a sermon on Sunday morning and then sit down at your dinner table before your family and criticize the minister, the sermon and everything at the church. Soon the children say to themselves, "What's the use? There isn't anything to religion." Years later you try to get them to attend church and they have no taste for it. You have allowed

Satan to use you. The Word was sown but you helped to pluck it out.

We ought to dust off our Bible and read it every day and resolve that we are going to use it wisely in His service. Yes, if I were Satan I would hinder God's Word.

IV. IF I WERE SATAN I WOULD TRY TO DESTROY THE POWER OF THE CHURCHES

He knows that one of the best ways to destroy the power of a church is to start a quarrel within a church. "Whom the gods would destroy they first make mad." The Jerusalem church was flourishing; Satan tried persecution; but the church still grew. Then he said, "I will start a quarrel on the inside." Some of the people began to murmur over the neglect of certain widows, and in a little while the church had a quarrel on its hands.

Ephesians 5:25: "Christ loved the church, and gave himself for it." He loves the Church more than any man loves his bride. He said, "I will build my Church." The Church must be of God or it would not have survived the years. It goes on and on even though it is built of poor human material, because God is behind it.

Jesus told one church that "it was neither hot nor cold." The Devil likes such a church. Heat is healing and cold is health-giving, but a lukewarm thing is useless and tasteless. Billy Sunday said that he knew some churches that were so cold you could skate down the aisles on the ice. Yes, the Devil does all he can to destroy the power of the churches — and he has succeeded in many places. God help us to keep preaching and teaching and praying and giving and living and serving so that our church might be a great power for Christ. If I were Satan I would try to destroy the power of the churches.

V. If I Were Satan I Would Make the Church Members Stumble

He keeps many from Christ this way. You, a Christian, may have working by your side a man who is not a Christian. One day you stumble and do an unchristian thing; then in ridicule the unsaved man says, "There is a Christian for you. If that is a sample of Christianity I want none of it."

A certain man said to me the other day, "One man kept me out of the church for twenty-five years. He was a big man in the church on Sunday but during the week he was a crook." Let me say this to you: do not let a hypocrite keep you out of the church. If you hide behind a hypocrite you are smaller than he is. The issue is between you and God. You must account for yourself to God and not for anyone else in the world. No matter what any puny little church member does or says, just remember that you must face God one day and you are to be careful how you live.

In the railroad yards you can find a little thin-edged rail by the side of the big rail. It is this small rail which sends the train to the side track. So Satan often uses a small thing to cause you to sin and to get off the right track. He knows that if he does cause you to stumble it will hurt the cause of Christianity.

A contractor is building a house and when the house is only half finished a man comes out to look it over. "Is that the best you can do?" he says to the contractor. "There is no roof on the house and look how rough everything is. You are not much of a contractor." Is this reasonable? No, we do not judge a contractor until the house is completed. You see a Christian with many faults, but you are not to judge him yet. Wait until God gets through with him and you will see a spotless saint standing before the throne. The difference in the Christian and the unbeliever is seen at the end of the way.

They may look alike now, but one day they will be totally different.

But we have a duty to the stumbler. We find it in Galatians 6:1: "Brethren, if a man be overtaken in a fault, ye which are spiritual, restore such an one in the spirit of meekness; considering thyself, lest thou also be tempted." The word "restore" here means to "reset". Just as an orthopedic surgeon resets a broken bone, so it is that when one stumbles and falls we are to tenderly put them back in place. But if I were Satan I would make church members stumble.

VI. If I Were Satan I Would Try to Give The World Another Gospel

The Devil does not care if you are religious and go to church, if you will just leave out the one saving element — the atonement of Christ and His blood as a covering for sin. Thousands of preachers today are preaching this bloodless Gospel. They talk of world peace and preservation of democracy and the good neighbor policy. These things are all right in their place, but these men have not one word to tell men that they are lost sinners and that Christ can save them for time and eternity.

Galatians 1:8: "Though we, or an angel from heaven, preached any other gospel unto you than that which we have preached unto you, let him be accursed." Today Satan is preaching another Gospel. What is the logic that he uses?

He preaches that God is too good to allow a man to be lost. He is just saying that a man can go ahead and live as he pleases, defying God and trampling Christ under foot. Since God is too good to punish him, God will give him a seat at the banquet table of heaven. My Bible does not teach me that and reason does not tell me so.

Satan preaches that a man should be good and honest and

treat his family well, and thus shall he be saved. We are not saved by our own goodness. "By grace are ye saved through faith; and that not of yourselves" (Eph. 2:8). He preaches that a man should join a church and then forget all about this matter of salvation. There are many who have done that, and apparently they know nothing of the saving grace of Christ. Jesus did not say that church membership would save. He did say, "Ye must be born again" (John 3:7).

The Devil preaches that everyone is going to be saved. But Daniel says, "Many of them that sleep in the dust of the earth shall awake, some to everlasting life, and some to shame and everlasting contempt" (Dan. 12:2). But the Devil is getting many men to preach his doctrine of universal salvation today.

Today there are some who are trying to preach a Gospel that has stood the test of the centuries — the pure Gospel of Jesus Christ. But many modernists are saying, "We do not believe this old stuff. Give us the Gospel for today." Believe me, my friends, this is the Gospel for today. It is the hope for today. Some things never change. The Gospel is the same always, but it is just as modern as tomorrow.

I sit on a great rock at the edge of a swirling river several hundred feet above the falls. Some men go by on a raft. They are headed toward the falls and they cry out to me, "Come on and ride with us." But I reply to them, "No, thank you, I am safe on this rock." Jesus Christ is the Rock of Ages. When a man asks me to trust something else I tell him that is is not safe. I am going to stay with Jesus. But if I were Satan I would try to get men to believe in a false Gospel.

VII. If I Were Satan I Would Get Men to Give Excuses

Jesus said to one man, "One thing thou lackest" (Mark 10:21). Usually it is not a multitude of things that keeps us away from Christ, but just one thing. And Satan keeps that excuse ever fresh in our minds to keep us from being saved.

Some man loves his money and he says, "I will be forced to give up too much to become a Christian." A man in New York said to a preacher, "If I become a Christian I must give up my business." The preacher answered, "It's a matter of giving up your business or your soul, which shall it be?" Some choose money and have it for a while, but they can not take it with them. If you choose Christ you will have salvation and joy in this life and when death comes your good times will have just begun.

The Devil's chief weapon is this: "You have plenty of time." He lets a man believe that there is a God, that Christ is Divine, that there is a judgment and eternity is coming; but he tells that man to wait a little while, to put the matter off. And while that man delays in making his decision, death slips upon him and he goes out into the other world doomed forever. Yes, if I were Satan I would fill the minds of men with excuses and watch them drift toward the Lake of Fire.

A Unitarian preacher sat by his fireside one cold night. He heard a knock at the door. When he opened it a little ragged girl said to him, "Please, sir, come and help me get my mother in." The preacher thought the mother must be drunk. He said "That is a job for the policeman. Go and get him." But the little girl said, "Oh, you don't understand! She is dying and I want you to come and get her in before she dies!" The preacher had no message for her, but the girl insisted and finally he went on with her.

He went into the poorly furnished room, sat down by the bed and talked about the golden rule and the moral ethical teachings of the Bible, but the poor woman cried out, "That is not for the likes of me! I cannot go back over my life and do those things. Don't you have a message for a woman who is dying without hope?" And then the preacher's mind went back to the old, old story of the Cross, which his mother had told him when he was a child. Soon he was telling the poor dying woman of One who died on Calvary and who would take her in if she came to Him. The old face lighted up with a smile and she said, "That is the message for the likes of me." She died, trusting in Jesus and rejoicing in salvation.

In telling about it later the preacher said, "Yes, I got her in. But that is not all — I went in too." And always after that he had a message in his heart.

This old, old message of Jesus and His Love is the message that the world needs. Are you in? Do not let Satan deceive you any longer. Come in today!